The Harvard Guide to Careers

THE
HARVARD GUIDE
TO
CAREERS

Martha P. Leape and Susan M. Vacca

New Edition

Distributed for the Office of Career Services
Faculty of Arts and Sciences, Harvard University
by Harvard University Press
Cambridge, Massachusetts
1991

Library of Congress Cataloging-in-Publication Data

Leape, Martha P.
　　The Harvard guide to careers / Martha P. Leape and Susan M. Vacca.—New ed.
　　　p. cm.
　　Includes bibliographical references and index.
　　ISBN 0-674-37565-3
　　1. Vocational guidance—United States.　2. Job hunting—United States.
3. Vocational guidance—United States—Bibliography.　4. Vocational
guidance—United States—Information services.　I. Vacca, Susan M., 1954- .
II. Title.
HF5382.5.U5L36　1991
331.7'02—dc20　　　91-3671
　　　　　　　　　CIP

Preface

This approach to career development has evolved from our work with Harvard College students and alumni, and with graduate students and Ph.D.'s in the Graduate School of Arts and Sciences. Their questions and concerns have challenged us to develop the resources and programs described in this book. In sharing their search for rewarding careers, we have gained insights into the processes of career exploration, career decision making, and job hunting.

This new edition contains greatly expanded and completely revised annotated bibliographies, updated sample letters and resumes, and a new section on financial planning.

Karen From designed and produced the book, with the assistance of Karen Cardozo Kane. We are grateful for their patience and persistence in helping us meet deadlines.

The pronouns *he*, *him*, and *his* are used throughout the book to denote a person of either sex. We are involved in serving the career development needs of both women and men, and this book is intended to speak to them all.

M.P.L.
S.M.V.

Contents

Chapter 1

CAREER EXPLORATION

INTRODUCTION

Some people let their careers happen by chance. They wait for opportunities to present themselves and take advantage of them as best they can. Others let someone else make decisions for them. They follow the career path that is recommended to them by a parent, a friend, or a teacher.

Some people take charge of their futures and forge their own careers. These individuals seek to understand their own unique interests, values, and abilities. They explore a wide range of possibilities and develop opportunities that enable them to use their talents to make a worthwhile contribution to society. Taking charge of one's future and making one's own career choices can be an exciting adventure.

As you undertake career exploration, it is not necessary or desirable to make a lifetime career choice. It may be that the career field that you choose now will be the field that you will work within for the rest of your working life. Or it may be that with time your values and interests will change and you will shift to a different field of work. Careers can be like the digging of a canal: steady progress along a well-defined and predetermined channel. Or they can be like trees growing and developing into unique shapes as they reach for the sun.

To find work that gives you the opportunity to work toward objectives that you value and challenges you to develop your talents, you need information about yourself: your values, interests, abilities, and goals. You also need information about career fields: the tasks, people, work environments, social impact, and rewards. By integrating information about yourself and about careers, you will be able to set priorities and evaluate options and thus make informed and intelligent choices.

Career Development, a Lifelong Process

Career development is a lifelong process, a series of options, hurdles, and decision points. There are those who believe the myth that one decision made early in life can determine an individual's lifework. This is not the reality that you will discover as you study other people's careers. You will find that most people make a series of career decisions which result in a variety of work experiences, adding up to something that they call their career.

Careers develop from the interaction of an individual's particular talents and personality with the responsibilities and tasks that he undertakes. In this process there are many options and many decision points along the way. Some of the decisions that you make will influence the course of your life more than others. No one decision, however, will determine what your work will be for the rest of your life.

If you are an undergraduate, your decision to seek a liberal education was an important one. The many decisions that you make during college about selection of concentration, elective courses, and extracurricular activities will shape your intellectual and personal development and your world view. Summer jobs and part-time volunteer or paid work during termtime also provide opportunities to learn about various career fields. You may decide to take a leave of absence, perhaps because you are offered a great job or perhaps because you want to be away from the pressures of the academic environment. When you are on your own in the working world, you will learn a great deal about the day-to-day realities of working and living. Many students have experiences during summers or leaves that introduce them to a career field which they decide to pursue after graduation.

If you are a graduate student, you made an important educational decision when you decided to earn a Ph.D. in your chosen field. Some of the factors in this decision were your enthusiasm for your subject, your love of scholarship and intellectual challenge, and your attraction to the academic environment. If you are reading this book, it is probably because you are interested in learning about the diversity of careers that you might pursue both inside and outside the university. People with Ph.D.'s enter many sectors of the world of work and are able to make special contributions because of their well-disciplined intellectual talents. Books like *Careers in Information* and *Corporate PhD* are testimony to this phenomenon. (See the bibliography at the end of this chapter for additional resources.)

Career Patterns

Most of you will probably have several occupations during your lifetime; either concurrently or serially, you will undertake different responsibilities. You might become a teacher and plan to reserve the school vacation times for writing poetry, or you might work for the television industry in a management position and use your personal time for writing scripts or plays or novels. You might develop a real estate business and, at the same time, serve in the state legislature.

Rather than pursue two occupations at one time, however, you may make career field changes from time to time. Even when changing fields, most people's career paths have continuity. They use the expertise gained in one position as preparation for the responsibilities they take on in the next. For example, a young woman who had become an officer in a commercial bank decided to make a change to the academic environment and became the financial officer of a college. A young faculty member in a history department decided to look for new opportunities to use his research and writing skills and, after a thorough search and a carefully planned job hunt, was hired by a large corporation to write a history of the corporation.

You may choose a complete career shift at some point. Career changes are happening more frequently today than ever before, as people seek a vocation that fulfills their goals and fits their lifestyles. Your enthusiasm for your first career field may decrease after some full-time experience, and you may decide you want to find a totally new occupation. It takes courage to make such a change. If, as a young person, you have learned how to develop career alternatives, and experienced the excitement of placing yourself in new and different environments, you are much more likely to have the courage to make a career change. The likelihood that your career will be a series of positions that are challenging and rewarding will be greatly increased if you learn how to engage actively in the development of your own career.

Career Exploration Timetable

Your schedule for exploring careers will depend on how close you are to a time when you would like to make a decision. If you are a freshman, you have four years ahead of you to learn about the world around you and to think about what kind of contribution you want to make. You can plan a variety of experiences to gather information that will help you formulate both short-term and long-term goals. Each year, through extracurricular activities, termtime internships, part-time work, volunteer activities, summer jobs, or perhaps employment during a leave of absence, you add to your knowledge about the world of work and about yourself. If you are a freshman considering one of the few career fields with undergraduate course requirements, you may want to undertake activities and experiences which will help you evaluate that career goal early in your college years.

If you are a junior or senior and wish to make a decision about what employment or graduate study to pursue after graduation, you may want to collect information more intensively. In this case, plan to spend several hours a week reading, talking to people, and becoming involved in career-related experiences which will help you move towards a decision. If you have already graduated from college, it will probably be advisable for you to find a job to support yourself while you gather information that enables you to make decisions about your career.

If you are a graduate student and want to learn about the variety of career opportunities for Ph.D.'s, you may design career exploration experiences that can be integrated into your graduate program. If teaching is not an expected part of your program, you may want to apply to be an instructor to develop teaching skills. If you have not had administrative or management experience, you may want to offer to take responsibility for planning the departmental colloquia or for administering some part of the academic or advising program. If you are curious about career opportunities outside the university, you may want to identify some Ph.D.'s whom you can visit at work for information interviews, as described below, to test your interest in different work environments. You might want to arrange an internship or short-term job outside the university. In addition, broadening your academic program, perhaps by taking some electives in a professional school, can be intellectually challenging and rewarding. You may even find that considering your long-range career interests in combination with your present academic interests helps you choose a thesis topic of more lasting intellectual and personal interest.

When you choose to take time to learn about career opportunities and to begin making career decisions is very much a personal matter. Some students focus all their energy on the opportunities for personal and intellectual growth during their college and graduate school programs. If, however, having a long-range career goal is important to you so that you may make other decisions in the context of that goal, you will want to engage in researching careers and expanding the variety of your work experiences while you are a student.

Academic Plans

Many undergraduates assume that they must choose their career goals before they can select a concentration. This is not true. You do not need, for example, to major in economics to get a job in business. Nor do you need to major in science to get into medical school or major in applied math to get a job in the computer science industry. Law schools accept candidates from all concentrations.

Your choice of major should be based on your intellectual interests. What are you excited about studying? What do you want to know more about? With which faculty members would you like to take further course work?

The Ph.D. program requires years of intensive, highly focused study in a chosen field. However, during your program, you make decisions that determine the breadth of your knowledge and experience in your discipline. Generally, broadening your areas of expertise and having a variety of work experiences that enhance your professional development increases your career opportunities when you graduate.

There are some specific courses which may be taken as electives by undergraduates or graduate students which are particularly relevant for certain types of employment. If you are interested in employment in business and nonprofit management, take introductory courses in economics, computers, accounting, and statistics. If you are interested in being a helping professional or teacher, be sure you work some introductory psychology or education courses into your program. If you are interested in an international career, become fluent in one or more foreign languages, take electives in the economics and the politics of the region of your interest, and plan to spend time living and working abroad.

Upperclassmen and graduate students may wish to identify electives in the graduate professional schools in their areas of career interest. Well-chosen electives can give you an introduction to the basic concepts and skills of a career field.

Getting Started

As you undertake a career exploration program, you will be gathering information about yourself and information about careers simultaneously. While getting involved in career-related experiences, you should be aware of what you are learning about yourself and what you are learning about career fields. It is important to gather facts about each field that you explore, but it is equally important to recognize your feelings and reactions to the people and the environment in which that work takes place.

The most important step in learning to know yourself is learning to trust your self-perception. Learn to observe your own behavior. Take note of your feelings. Attend to your reactions and your everyday choices. Gather information from your friends, your family, and from people with whom you work. Their perceptions of you provide valuable data, but, remember, you are the best authority on you.

The best way to increase your knowledge of yourself in relation to the world of work is through exposure to different work environments. As you plan your career exploration, seek new experiences which will give you new information or reinforce old information about yourself. The following are some of the questions to ask yourself:

- To what kind of work do I want to commit my talents, time, and energy?
- What kind of work do I find challenging and rewarding?
- What special talents do I have?
- In what type of environment do I work best?
- What kinds of relationships with people do I value?
- Are the objectives or products of the organizations more important to me than my specific role?
- Is the social contribution of the work important to me?
- What priority do I give status, power, and level of income?
- How do my personal, educational, marriage, or family plans influence my career plans?

The best ways of gathering information about careers include:

- Reading biographical, occupational, and professional literature;
- Interviewing and spending time with people in their places of employment;

• Working as a volunteer or for pay in the work environment.

What you want to learn about the career fields you are exploring depends on what is important to you. The next section, "Career Dimensions," is an attempt to outline some of the many aspects of a career which you may want to think about during your career exploration and decision making.

CAREER DIMENSIONS

As you embark on career exploration, consider what is most important to you. The following discussion of career dimensions is presented to help you think about some of the characteristics of careers. This outline is not meant to be comprehensive, but is intended to stimulate you to devise your own outline of career dimensions.

Rewards System

Are the objectives of the work or of the organization important to you? If you can make a positive contribution to our society or to our world, is that more important to you than specific tasks you are required to do?

Is the social value of the outcome of your labors important to you? What priority do you give the social value of your work in relation to other rewards, such as income, or functions that you find challenging, or being in a particular geographic location?

Is public recognition or social status important to you? If you perform well in this career field, will you be respected and admired in your community? Will people in the community know about your achievements?

What is the income potential in this career field? What level of income would you expect in a starting position? What level of income would you expect in five years, ten years?

Whatever the daily functions of this career, do you think they would be satisfying to you? Would you enjoy the doctor-patient relationship, the teacher-student relationship, the lawyer-client relationship? Would you feel rewarded by solving an important business problem or by designing a plan for marketing a new product, by assisting a new employee, or by becoming the leader of a team?

Is there opportunity for the personal satisfaction of creating something? Is there opportunity to think about problems and processes and to design new solutions?

Work Tasks and Functions

Does the work involve primarily organizing and processing data, building and operating equipment, or discovering, analyzing, and writing about ideas? What kinds of problem solving does the work require? Is a major portion of time spent in analysis and checking accuracy of details, or in the synthesis and development of ideas and plans?

What kinds of decision making does the job require? Is it possible to know all the pertinent facts before having to make a decision? Is it necessary to make decisions based on very little information? Does the job require taking risks? Does the job require dealing with uncertainty?

Does the job involve working with people in helping relationships, team relationships, persuasive relationships, or supervisory relationships? Is the worker seen primarily as a person who helps others?

Is the problem solving or policy development focused on the local community, the larger U.S. community, another country or region, the global community? Will the results of the work impact on the welfare of a few people, many people, all people?

Does the worker have his own job to do, or is the completion of his work dependent on the work of others? Does the work involve influencing and persuading others? Does the work involve telling others what to do?

Work Styles

Is the job tightly defined so that you know not only what you are supposed to do, but how you are supposed to do it? Is the job loosely defined, stating only objectives, so that you may design the process of achieving the objectives? Are you given autonomy in how you achieve objectives?

Is it possible to do this work on a self-employed basis? Would working for yourself, on your own time, be suitable for you?

What is the pace of the work? Can you plan your week's work ahead of time or is it unevenly paced, with unexpected new assignments with urgent deadlines, and slow times when there is little to do?

What are the hours that you are expected to work? Do most people in this field work from nine to five, or eight to six, or seven to seven? Do the people in this career work five or six or seven days a week? Do the hours tend to be irregular, with long hours expected at certain times of year?

How much variety is there in the work? Are the tasks and responsibilities different from one day to the next, from one hour to the next? Are there new types of problems to be solved? Is it the kind of job that, once you have a basic amount of experience, you can approach each day with confidence, feeling comfortable that you can accomplish what is expected of you?

Does the job require cautious, deliberative decision making? Is there time for careful research and analysis before making decisions? Or does the job require quick, even spontaneous, decisions?

Work Environment

Physical and Geographical Environment

What is the personal work space like? If the work takes place primarily at a desk, will that desk be in a large and spacious office which seems to communicate status and success, or will that desk be one with a computer terminal in the middle of the city room with fellow reporters tapping out stories on all sides of you? Will your personal work space be an unimportant factor because you will be spending most of your day in other places?

Is the job likely to be in a rural setting or in a large city? Will your working day be spent indoors or outdoors or some combination of both?

Will the work permit you to continue living in one place? Or will you be required, expected, or allowed to move from city to city, from country to country?

Does the job require travel? Will you have frequent business trips to interesting places? Will you spend most of your time away from your home base or most of your time in your home office? Will you have extended trips or international trips?

Will the work require that you live overseas for short periods of time, for several years, for most of your career?

Organizational Environment

Is the organization highly structured, with clear definition of authority lines? Are the job descriptions explicit and detailed? Are the expectations clear? Does the supervisor pay attention to the details and daily progress of your work?

Is the organization loosely structured? Are the responsibilities defined in terms of objectives rather than in terms of the details of how the objective should be reached? Is the worker given little instruction and supervision and expected to devise his own way of fulfilling his responsibilities?

Is there opportunity for advancement? Is it clear what the criteria are for earning promotions? Does this organization tend to promote inside candidates or hire from outside?

Human Environment

Are the relationships with fellow workers best characterized as competitive, collaborative, or cooperative? Do employees work alone on their own projects and compete with one another, or do they collaborate toward common goals? Does the job require working in interdependent relationships with others in order to fulfill one's responsibilities?

What kind of contacts, if any, does the worker have with people outside the organization? If a job requires meeting people, would the purpose of the meeting be to help the client with a personal problem, to help the client with a professional problem, to teach the person something, to negotiate a contract, or to sell the person a product or a service?

If the organization is a service organization, what kind of population does it serve: old people, young people, rich people, poor people, sick people, people who have serious personal problems? Do you want to work with the population which the agency serves?

If the organization produces a product, do employees work in teams or is their function independent of others? Is the contribution of each individual identifiable?

Some of the characteristics in this outline may not seem important to you. There may be other characteristics not mentioned that you will discover are very important to you.

Design your own outline to represent your view of the important dimensions of careers. You can use your outline to identify the characteristics of the career fields you are exploring and to analyze what you have learned about your personal preferences and priorities. As your insight into what characteristics are important to you increases, the task of making a career choice, even though it may be a tentative choice, becomes possible.

IDENTIFYING CAREERS TO EXPLORE

You may have a career goal which you have had in mind for some time. If so, your first objective in career exploration is to learn more about that career and evaluate the opportunities that it offers you.

If you have not had a long-range career goal, the process of arriving at a list of careers to explore is your first opportunity to practice career decision making. Match what you know about yourself from your past experiences with a list of career fields that you recognize as possible choices. Make a list of four or five careers for your initial exploration. Bear in mind that as you expand your experiential knowledge of careers, you will at the same time be expanding your knowledge of yourself. Your list of career alternatives will be continually evolving.

You have many resources from which to generate a list of careers which you might explore. The following resources are some of the most helpful.

Generating a List

Recommendations of Teachers and Parents. People who know you well and care about you may have ideas about what career fields you would enjoy. Do not ignore their suggestions. Although you may think that their perceptions of you are inaccurate, incomplete, or outdated, it may be worth testing out their recommendations with some research and career-related experiences.

Recommendations of Friends. During your years as a student, you have been working and living with peers who know you well. Have you asked your friends and roommates what career they think you would enjoy? They may suggest a career that you have not considered.

Daydreams. When you dream about the future, what kind of work do you see yourself doing? What kind of role do you have in your community? What kind of organization do you work for? When you were twelve years old and thought about being an adult, what kind of career did you envision? If you haven't taken time to dream about the future recently, set aside some time when you can be by yourself in a relaxed and comfortable place and try to visualize your life ten years hence.

Lists of Occupations. There are many reference books which describe jobs and careers. Scanning the job titles listed in these books and reading about those that spark your curiosity helps you to expand your career horizons. *The American Almanac of Jobs and Salaries* and the *Occupational Outlook Handbook* are good places to start, as are the Catalyst Career

Opportunity Series and VGM Opportunities Series. If you are fascinated by high technology, but are not sure of your skills, take a look at *High-Tech Jobs for Non-Tech Grads*. Are you feeling that your creative side needs expression? You'll enjoy reading *Creative Careers*. If you are concerned about the environment, peruse *The Complete Guide to Environmental Careers*. *Careers for Dreamers and Doers: A Guide to Management Careers in the Nonprofit Sector* could lead you to an interesting career with a public service organization.

Learning From Past Experiences

Thinking analytically about past activities and events that were satisfying and rewarding can be helpful in identifying careers you might enjoy. Try the following exercises.

I. Make a list of eight to ten accomplishments of which you are proud. Do not limit your list to achievements recognized by others; include achievements which you feel were milestones in your own development or important contributions to those around you.

   A. Answer the following questions about each incident:

   • Why do you feel proud of this achievement?
   • What were the rewarding and frustrating aspects of this experience?
   • What talents and abilities did it require?

   B. When you have answered these questions about each experience, ask yourself the following:

   • Do these achievements have any common themes such as similar challenges, rewards, or objectives?
   • Do they require similar skills?
   • Do these characteristics seem related to any particular careers?

II. Make a list of school, college, or community organizations of which you have been a member in recent years. Becoming aware of the roles in which you are most comfortable and productive in organizations can be helpful in planning your career exploration.

A. Describe your role in each of these groups.

- Describe your relationship to the other members of the group and to the "work" of the group.
- List the positions of responsibility to which you were elected, appointed, and volunteered for in each group.

B. When you have answered these questions, look for common themes in your behavior as a group member.

- Do you usually take on group leadership responsibilities, organizing, scheduling, and delegating the work to be done?
- Or are you more inclined to seek a role in which you can make a contribution, but not be responsible for the work of others?
- Are you the person who initiates new activities, the person from whom others seek advice, or the person who makes sure that everyone feels included?

Thinking analytically about your past enables you to identify the characteristics of work that are important to you and to begin to list your work values, interests, and skills. Chapter 2 will discuss career decision making in greater detail and will list some sources that can guide you through this process.

Vocational Interest Inventories

Vocational interest inventories can provide information that gives you new insights and assists you in evaluating what you have learned from your past experiences. The inventory asks you questions about your preferences and what you like to do, and, from this information, a profile of your interests is generated. Your interest profile is then correlated with the profiles of people in different occupations. This information can help you select fields that are important to you. These tests will not give you information about your abilities, only about your interests and values.

Discussion with a counselor about vocational interest inventories will help you identify careers to explore and also suggest some of the characteristics of career fields that are important to you.

Working With a Career Counselor

By listening to the thoughts and feelings that you express about yourself, your past experiences, and your future, a career counselor may be able to help you gain new and clearer insight into what you have to offer and what you are looking for in your career. Your career counselor can help you translate what you have learned from your past experiences into career-related skills and characteristics. If you have already identified several careers which you wish to explore, your career counselor will help you to outline a plan for experiential research. If you do not yet have a list of careers to explore, that will be your first objective.

What is the best way to find a career counselor? Your college or university career office should be your first stop. Many institutions offer counseling not only for currently enrolled students, but also for alumni. If your college does not have such services available to you, visit your local public library. A reference librarian should be able to help you to identify local organizations that offer career guidance or can refer you to directories like the *Directory of Counseling Services* or the *National Directory of Career Resource Centers*.

There are career and vocational counselors in private practice. Some advertise in local newspapers or can be found in the Yellow Pages; others will be recommended to you by friends.

Evaluate a career counselor as you would any other professional from whom you seek services: ask for credentials; be clear about what your objectives are and what kind of assistance you need. Recognize that personalities are a factor—you may or may not be comfortable with a particular personality or approach to career planning. After all, you are a unique person with your own desires and needs. Be sure to ask in advance what the services will cost.

Your Career Research File

Careful records are essential to keeping track of your career research. Whether you use a card file, folders, or notebooks is your choice, but you must be able to organize information by career field.

It is advisable to take notes on everything you read and to make lists of people you would like to contact. Keep copies of all your correspondence and record dates and notes on all telephone calls. After each interview, make notes of information you learned, the observations you made, and the impressions you formed. You may want to keep a journal about your experiences and reactions.

The next three sections discuss three different sources of information about careers: reading materials such as books, pamphlets, magazines, and newspapers; people in the careers that you are exploring; and short-term jobs or internships.

USING CAREER LITERATURE

What's Out There?

When you start your career exploration, you will probably have some ideas about what possibilities exist out there in the "real world." You may even be very familiar with the specifics of a field or two. But what about the rest of the possibilities in the world of work? What about those areas of employment you've never heard of, or whose names conjure a fuzzy image in your mind? How do you go about getting more information about them? You do something you're probably very good at by now: you research!

No matter how busy you are with your current activities, arrange to spend some time reading about careers and about people in different professions. This is an investment of time that will pay for itself many times over. You will learn about what people find interesting and rewarding in their chosen work. From reading the journals and magazines they read, you will learn about the problems and issues that concern professionals in different fields and will acquaint yourself with their vocabularies and styles of expression. More importantly, you will find yourself beginning to identify aspects of professions that you like or dislike.

Where Do You Start?

Try the annotated bibliographies at the end of each chapter in this book, but pay special attention to those at the end of this chapter. The sources listed under the headings "Career Descriptive Literature," "Directories of Career Literature and Counselors," and "Directories of Trade and Professional Journals and Associations" will become valued companions in this search and, most likely, in any later career exploration you do. The more you use these references, the more comfortable you will be with them, and the more information you will be able to extract from each one. In fact, these are the sources that were used to research the career fields described in the second part of this chapter.

If you are interested in going abroad or working in the sphere of international relations, *Careers in International Affairs* or *International Jobs: Where They Are, How to Get Them* will prove invaluable to you.

The bibliographies provide you with examples of the kinds of information to look for and the likely sources for finding it. Read through the sampling of career fields; follow up with some of the items in the bibliographies. Scan the "Index of Resources by Career Field" in the Appendix. If you don't find the exact career field you're looking for, pick something that might be related. Then refer back to this chapter's bibliographies to get a start: the *Occupational Outlook Handbook* and subject guide to *Books in Print* should launch you.

What Next?

Consult one of the periodical directories. *The Gale Directory of Publications and Broadcast Media*, although of particular interest to someone wishing to enter the magazine publishing field, will provide the names of trade and professional journals in a wide range of fields, enabling you to begin reading what the professionals read in the field you are exploring. The journals may have interesting book reviews and may be sprinkled with the names of people prominent in the field. Find out more about these individuals by checking biographical dictionaries and directories, which you identify by using *Directories in Print*.

Directories in Print will prove useful to you again later in your search when you want to identify potential employers in a particular field. For instance, here you will find a reference to *Consultants and Consulting Organizations Directory* (listed in the bibliography at the end of Chapter 3), which will enable you to find out who does management consulting, health care consulting, environmental consulting, or consulting in any number of specialized areas. It will also help you to identify what the possibilities are in the world of consulting and to match those opportunities against your own subject strengths and interests.

Is This Really as Complicated and Confusing as It Sounds?

It doesn't have to be. The key to using career literature and other reference materials to your advantage in your career exploration is to maintain an open mind and to follow up on the interesting facts you discover. This is where your career research file proves its worth. Jot down the name of the professional association that's mentioned in the newspaper article you have in front of you. Later on, you can consult the *Encyclopedia of Associations* to get an address or phone number and to see if the group publishes a newsletter or journal.

You will develop certain habits almost subconsciously—for instance, reading the *Wall Street Journal* or other trade or professional publications with pen and pad close by so that you can jot down the names of interesting companies or organizations. While scanning articles for names of individuals prominent in a particular field, you will come across a job title you've never seen before. The quest for more information about this job in the *Occupational Outlook Handbook* will lead you to related or similar positions. The titles on organizational culture at the end of Chapter 4 may help you to decide what kind of setting you would find most compatible with your interests, or, perhaps more important, what kinds of organizations hold no appeal for you.

Does It Ever End?

Probably not. After you have secured your first position, you will continue to explore the paths open to you. As you have new experiences and increase your areas of expertise, your career interests will continue to develop. As your life changes, so will your career priorities. You may find yourself moving from the private sector to the public or nonprofit sector, and then back again. Geography may become a factor if you are in a two-career relationship, causing you to confine your explorations to a certain part of the country or to relocate to another area. If so, directories with geographic indexes will facilitate your search.

As you refine your career research skills and allow your imagination to lead you, possibilities will continue to unfold. When you combine your "book learning" with visiting and interviewing career advisers, the differences of the dimensions of each career will become clearer to you.

INTERVIEWING CAREER ADVISERS

People are the best source of information about careers. Careers do not exist as objective phenomena which become superimposed on a person's life. The responsibilities and requirements of a particular position influence the daily life of the person, but each individual meets those demands and responsibilities differently and thereby develops a career experience which is unique. To get a personal view of how someone is developing his career and what he finds rewarding in his work, you must interview him. Most people, even busy people, enjoy talking with a young person about their careers.

It is preferable to visit people at work so that you may observe the activities, the environment, and the human community in which the work takes place. It is likely that the person you are interviewing will give more realistic information and impressions about his work if interviewed on the job than in a social setting.

Identifying People to Visit

The career offices of many colleges have files of the names of alumni who have volunteered to serve as career advisers. These women and men are valuable sources of information and advice about their profession or their geographic location.

Career panels held by college career offices and by other career services are an excellent way to meet people who might be interesting career advisers for you. If you are particularly interested in a speaker on a career panel, try to speak him after the meeting to set up a time for an individual conference. If it is not possible to talk with the speaker at the meeting, find out his name and address from the host so that you can write to request an opportunity to meet.

There are many special visitors at a university each year. Some stay for only a few days, others stay for a full academic year. When you learn about a person coming as a lecturer or a guest performer in the arts, contact the office hosting the visitor ahead of time to see if there will be an opportunity for you to have an individual conference with that person. Even if this introductory interview is brief, the visitor may agree to have you visit him at work to learn more about his career field.

Visiting Fellows are often interested in getting to know students. They usually accept with enthusiasm invitations to come to your dining hall for lunch or dinner. If you take the initiative to become acquainted with Visiting Fellows early in the year, you may find that by the end of the year you have made a friend who is established in a career field that interests you and can give you very pertinent career advice and assistance in your job hunt.

Another source of career advisers is hometown friends, and parents and friends of your roommates. You can arrange to meet these people at work when you are at home or when visiting a roommate during vacations. Even if this friend is the person who lives next door, it is preferable that your interview for career advice take place at his office rather than in your home.

Local alumni groups are an excellent place to start; you can also identify potential career advisers from people mentioned in professional journals and magazines and authors of articles that interest you. There are directories listing people in almost every line of work: the title index in *Directories in Print* lists several columns of titles beginning with "Who's Who in . . ." Then there are the "industry" directories, like *Editor and Publisher International Yearbook, The Rand McNally Banker's Directory*, or the *National Directory of Children and Youth Services* which give names of officers as well as names and addresses of organizations. Letters to these people stating that you are interested in their career field and asking if you can meet with them at their place of work are very likely to receive positive responses. Be sure to make it clear that you are not asking for a job; you are seeking information and advice that will help you make a career decision.

Preparing for an Information Interview

It is important that you read occupational literature and professional publications of the adviser's career field before you visit him. If the adviser works for a large corporation or organization, locate an annual report of the organization. If the adviser works in the federal government in Washington, look up his name in the *Federal Executive Directory* to find out his title and position, and research his agency in *The United States Government Manual*. If he is a member of Congress, you will find a list of his committee memberships in *The Almanac of American Politics*, *Politics in America*, or the *Congressional Yellow Book*.

If you're planning to visit an adviser at an advertising agency, check the *Standard Directory of Advertising Agencies* to see what accounts his firm handles. *Literary Market Place* will tell you what kinds of books a publisher publishes. *Public Interest Profiles* describes the activities and political orientation of organizations involved in public policy matters, from environmental groups to think tanks. In short, show the adviser that you cared enough to do some research!

It is advisable to prepare a resume to take with you when you visit career advisers. If you hand the adviser a resume at the beginning of the interview to introduce yourself, he does not need to ask you about your background. You may proceed directly with the questions which you want to discuss about the adviser's career. For advice on writing resumes and sample resumes, see Chapter 4.

Planning What You Want to Learn From the Career Adviser

The most important benefit of an information interview is understanding another person's career experience. You want to learn what the career adviser finds rewarding in his work and what aspects are frustrating. As he shares with you what he has experienced as the reality in his chosen field, you will be able to sense whether his enthusiasm about his work stems primarily from his daily tasks and responsibilities, from the people with whom he works, from his commitment to the objectives of his work, or from financial or other rewards. The primary objective of your interview is to learn about the personal experiences of the adviser in his career including:

- the types of rewards he values,
- the challenges of his daily work,
- the programs he is developing,
- the problems he thinks about,
- the types of decisions he makes,
- his long-range and short-range objectives,
- his relations with co-workers and clients,
- the steps he took to arrive at his present position.

It is interesting to seek his advice on the best way to enter the field, on how to prepare for entry-level positions, on what reading will help increase your understanding of the field, and on part-time or short-term work experiences that will provide opportunities to evaluate your interest in his field.

Observing the Work Environment and the People

An important aspect of your visit to a career adviser is the opportunity to observe and react to the environment in which the adviser works. Do you like the physical surroundings? Perhaps the adviser will take you on a tour of the office so that you are able to meet other people and observe what they are doing. This exposure gives you an opportunity to see how people interact in the environment and to learn how the functions and tasks are divided up.

Take note of your reactions to every aspect of the situation. Do you find this an exciting place to be? Are the people interesting to you? Would you like to be doing what they are doing? Would you like your working life to be like theirs?

After the Visit

It is important to write a short letter of thanks to the career adviser after each interview. If some questions have occurred to you after the interview, feel free to ask them in this letter. If you plan to contact people whom he has recommended to you or to arrange experiences which he suggested, make sure you report your progress in a letter or a telephone call. Remember that each career adviser is a valuable human resource to you. Having shared some of his personal career experiences, he will be very interested in hearing from you periodically about how your career is developing.

After each interview, make notes for your career research file on the information and advice you have received, the observations you made of the work environment, and your reactions to the adviser and his work.

ARRANGING CAREER-RELATED EXPERIENCES

Spending time in the work place and observing or practicing the work functions and roles of a professional gives you information about the occupation and insights about yourself which you cannot learn from books.

Extracurricular Activities

In the college community, there are many opportunities to learn career-related skills and to test your career interests. You can determine whether you enjoy management responsibility by serving as the manager of a music organization or athletic team, or by producing a show. You can learn about advertising and marketing by being the business manager of a student publication or as a manager of a campus business or service. You can experience the excitement and frustrations of journalism by writing for a student newspaper. You can learn about instructing, advising, and evaluating people by being a tutor or teaching fellow. You can be a counselor to your fellow students as a member of a peer counseling group. You can have the experience of helping people in need or working toward improving society through peer counseling services or community service programs. You can participate in campus organizations related to politics and government, or you can become an active participant in student government and student/faculty advisory groups. A range of student organizations offer you the opportunity to develop career-related skills and to serve your college community at the same time.

Short-Term Jobs

Outside the university community, there are many opportunities for you to engage in short-term work experience. Summer jobs, leaves of absence, and part-time employment during the school year provide you with limited periods of time to arrange jobs which give you the opportunity to test yourself in a variety of different work environments. If you do a different kind of work each summer, you will learn a great deal about yourself and about career fields. Don't focus too early. Regard these opportunities for short-term work experience as "career electives" and try to experiment as broadly as possible. Plan at least one summer abroad.

It is true that in these work experiences you will not have the same responsibilities as you would have in a full-time position, but you will be able to experience the work environment. You gain the opportunity to observe at close range the daily tasks and interactions of professionals working in the field you might enter. For example, an orderly in a hospital has the opportunity to observe a doctor's interactions with patients and to observe how the behavior of the doctor affects both the patients and the staff. At the same time, the orderly fulfills some important functions in the care of patients. The management intern in business will not usually be given management responsibilities, but will be assigned projects that relate to management functions. The intern will also have the opportunity to observe the manager's daily activities.

If you are a graduate student, your time to plan "career electives" may be limited. If you become a residential adviser to undergraduates, you will have responsibility for advising and program development. If you apply to be an academic adviser, you will be given administrative responsibilities. If you are interested in exploring careers in the nonacademic world, in addition to taking related courses you should design some kind of short-term internships or jobs which will give you the opportunity to experience directly the functions and environments of other careers.

Career Exploration Opportunities With Varying Time Commitments

There are a variety of activities in which you can learn about careers which require different levels of commitment and different allotments of time. You may start at any time that suits your schedule and needs. Each type of activity offers you direct personal experience in a vocational field of your choice.

Interviewing Career Advisers. This is a good place to start. The time commitment is variable, and you can regulate the amount of time you spend in accordance with other demands on your time. Identify advisers whose careers interest you and make appointments by letter or by telephone. To prepare for the visit, read about the adviser's career field and organization so that you have some basic understanding of his work. Plan to arrive early so that you have some time to observe the work environment and perhaps chat with the receptionist. To introduce yourself, hand the adviser a copy of your resume and then lead off the conversation by inquiring what he finds rewarding in his work. This focuses the interview on the evaluation of rewards and usually generates a valuable interchange.

Shared Experience. By talking to career advisers or your career counselor, you may be able to identify someone whom you could visit several hours each week for a couple of months. During this time, you could either get hands-on experience by working on a particular project or you could shadow the professional for part of the time and then discuss your observations with him.

Termtime Internship/Job. If you are ready to arrange a larger time commitment for career exploration, perhaps ten to twenty hours per week, you can find opportunities which offer you more responsibility. There are clearinghouses and directories for internships and volunteer opportunities in government or in nonprofit public service, media, arts, health, and business. Some states and cities have offices that generate internship listings. In addition, the directories shown in the "Internships and Summer Work" section of the bibliography at the end of this chapter will help you to identify other resources.

Internships. These are often arranged individually. A career adviser or counselor may be able to help you identify people with whom you might be able to arrange a part-time volunteer experience. An unpaid internship during one semester can lead to paid part-time work or a paid summer job. Employers are inclined to hire for summer jobs people whom they know and who have already been doing work for them on an unpaid basis.

Short-Term Internships/Experiences. Some colleges or alumni clubs offer brief internships during college vacations which provide the opportunity for you to spend one to five days with a professional in a career field you are exploring. You can often arrange your own brief internships by expressing interest in spending a day or several days with a career adviser to learn the variety of activities, decisions, and interactions he engages in on a typical day.

Summer Job/Internship. College summers offer a special opportunity for short-term, full-time work experience in the U.S. or abroad. If you do not have to earn extra money, you can probably arrange almost any kind of experience anywhere in the world. If you need to earn money, as most students do, you should start early in the fall term to search for a paid summer job in the career field that you are exploring. If you are unable to find a paid opportunity, you may decide to take an unpaid part-time job in order to gain the experience in a field that interests you.

Books like *Getting Work Experience* will introduce you to summer internships and summer jobs, as will the special indexes in *Peterson's Job Opportunities for Business and Liberal Arts Graduates* and *Peterson's Job Opportunities for Engineering, Science and Computer Graduates* (listed in the bibliography at the end of Chapter 3). *Great Careers: The Fourth of July Guide to Careers, Internships, and Volunteer Opportunities in the Non-profit Sector* and *New Careers: A Directory of Jobs and Internships in Technology and Society* will lead you to summer opportunities in public and community service organizations. You can also identify potential employers by use of various industry or trade directories.

A summer job hunt should be conducted in the same way as any other job hunt. Chapter 4 contains advice on preparing your resume, writing cover letters, and interviewing with potential employers. Start early. Search broadly. Apply for a variety of opportunities.

Leave of Absence/Interim Employment. A leave of absence provides you with the opportunity to be a full-time responsible worker in an organization, and a self-supporting adult, perhaps in a new community or overseas. Because you commit yourself for a longer time, employers are usually willing to give you more responsibility.

You can start your job search by looking through internship directories to get ideas about opportunities that are available. You may apply for and get one of the internships listed. Or you might choose to arrange your own work opportunity, selecting a type of work you want to experience or a place you want to live. If you are persistent in your search, you will surely be able to arrange an interesting experience.

On your first job after graduation, you will continue to learn about yourself and about career characteristics to which you want to give priority. This process of career development will continue throughout your life.

ENRICHING YOUR EDUCATION WITH INTERNATIONAL EXPERIENCE

The adventure of working or studying abroad adds a special dimension to your education. Living in a foreign culture, learning different ways to meet daily needs and build relationships, trying to understand different ideas and concerns about national and international issues expands your awareness of the diversity of human communities. Being away from the culture in which you grew up provides the opportunity to see more clearly what you value and what you might like to work to improve in your own society. *The Harvard Guide to International Experience* is a good place to begin your research as you plan your overseas adventure.

If you spend time abroad, you will be challenged to be more independent than you have ever been before, a prospect that is as exciting as it is daunting. You will have the chance to prove to yourself that you can cope in new and different environments, that you can be adaptable and self-sufficient.

Depending on where you choose to go, you will experience varying degrees of cultural differences. You will have a chance to test your language skills or to learn a new language in a new way. You will find different ways of structuring work and the professions that help meet human needs. You will learn different expectations and customs regarding marriage, family, and community. Living and working or studying in another country is exciting and mind-expanding. Far from the comforts of familiar surroundings, you become involved in a new culture, learning new ways and new perspectives on life.

When Should I Go?

Your timing will be influenced by what you want to do. If you are an undergraduate, you may want to arrange an internship or job in a foreign country during the summer or a leave of absence for the year after graduation. You could volunteer to work in a mission hospital, in an orphanage, on an environmental education project, or in a development agency. The books listed in the "Work and Study Abroad" section of the bibliography at the end of this chapter will give you many ideas for activities to consider.

Many kinds of work opportunities are possible, such as teaching English, serving as a research assistant, or writing for an English-language newspaper, but you do have to inform yourself about work permit regulations. Short-term work permits may be obtained while you are a student or even as a graduating senior from the Council on International Educational Exchange.

If you decide to study at a foreign university, you can apply to one of the many programs sponsored by U.S. institutions or you can apply directly to the foreign university as a special student. At most colleges you can petition for degree credit for coursework done at another university. Because you will have to plan in advance when these activities will best fit into your academic program, it's never too soon to start thinking about where you would like to go and what you would like to study.

Another good time to arrange an experience abroad is after graduation. The internship or job you arrange might be directly or tangentially related to your career. It might be a time you set aside for a special experience in human service through the Peace Corps or some other international volunteer organization.

If you are a graduate student, time abroad can be spent doing thesis research and writing. There are predoctoral and postdoctoral fellowships and internships at foreign universities and in international organizations such as the United Nations. The funding references such as *Financial Aid for Research, Study, Travel, and Other Activities Abroad* and *Financial Resources for International Study: A Definitive Guide to Organizations Offering Awards for Overseas Study* listed in the "Work and Study Abroad" section of the bibliography will be of particular interest to you.

Learning about Foreign Opportunities. Deciding Where to Go.

Read everything you can and talk to as many people as you can. Find out who among your friends has been abroad and meet with them to discuss their experiences. Ask your instructors and career counselor for suggestions. Contact alumni of your college who live abroad or the officers of alumni clubs in foreign countries. Do all the things you would do if you were trying to find out about opportunities in the U.S.

Finally, be realistic. Choose an activity and location that will be enriching and challenging, but be aware of the adjustments you will have to make. Find out as much as you can about the work opportunity and responsibilities; about living arrangements, housing, diet, transportation, isolation from other Americans; and about programs for language training and orientation to the culture.

EXPANDING YOUR HORIZONS BY EXPERIENCING THE UNFAMILIAR

Whether the adventures you plan during your career exploration take you abroad or just into new "worlds" at home, you will expand your knowledge about careers by risking these new experiences. It takes courage to walk into a new job, to move to a new city, to begin work in a new environment where you don't know anybody. It can be a little scary, but the potential for learning about yourself and about new career options is worth some risk.

Taking on new responsibilities in unfamiliar surroundings is a way of testing yourself. New challenges allow you to discover talents and abilities that you did not know you had. Having to relate to different people in a new organization develops your understanding of individual differences. Experiencing new worlds of work expands your knowledge of the diversity of career opportunities.

Getting away from the familiar and comfortable helps increase your self-knowledge. Meeting the challenge of becoming productive in a new environment helps you identify new strengths and increases your self-confidence. Being separated from the people most significant to you provides the opportunity to see more clearly who you are, apart from and because of these relationships. Distance makes it possible to view the possibilities in your familiar surroundings more objectively.

The risks involved in adventures into new "worlds" can be minimized by careful research and preparation. From reading and from knowledgeable people you can become informed about customs, mores, and expectations. If you have the opportunity to talk in advance with people in the new organization, you can glean information and advice that will help you to get a good start in the new environment.

Unless you experiment in new "worlds," you are not really exploring! Don't cheat yourself of the excitement of risking new adventures. There are many resources that you can use to plan horizon-expanding adventures in this country and abroad. Those listed in the bibliography at the end of this chapter will give you a good start, as will the job-hunting resources at the end of Chapter 3. All you have to do is take the first step!

AN INTRODUCTION TO SELECTED CAREER FIELDS

The following are brief introductions to a few of the many career fields which can be entered without professional graduate education. These introductions illustrate differences in work styles, demands, rewards, objectives, and environments that characterize different careers. None of these descriptions is in any way comprehensive; there are entire books written about most of these fields.

The purpose of these profiles is to illustrate the diversity of career cultures, to introduce you to some of the characteristics of these cultures, and to provide examples of how to gather information about the careers that interest you.

We hope these glimpses of a few careers will whet your appetite to research careers through books and journals and through interviewing people at work. The objective of your search is to identify career opportunities that you will find challenging, satisfying, exciting, and rewarding.

Advertising

When you watch television, do you look at the ads? Are the ads sometimes more interesting and memorable than the TV program itself? Do you find yourself analyzing the effectiveness of the ads and thinking about ways that their appeal could be improved?

Do you read ads in magazines? Are you impressed with the imaginativeness with which they present their messages? Do you think that you could do it more creatively? Would you like to try?

Maybe you would be interested in a career in advertising. Advertising is creative; it is competitive. It is the business of promoting the products of your client's company over all others. Creativity is highly valued in advertising, but so is the ability to listen, to articulate ideas, and to work productively with others.

People in advertising thrive on the challenge of developing a better idea than their competitors. They study marketing strategies, consumer habits, media programming, and ratings. When they create an advertising campaign, they design messages for a target population with a defined objective. Change in market share for their client's product is the criterion by which their work is judged.

Advertising is in a period of rapid change. With the development of new communications technology, the number and variety of methods and media being used in creating, producing, and distributing messages is growing rapidly. Television, the primary advertising revenue producer, is experiencing a falloff in ad sales for the first time ever. Advertising executives are increasingly challenged to explore new ways to get their message to the public, utilizing such media as direct mail, cable TV, catalog and sales services, and magazine chain ads.

With the dramatic changes in research capabilities using computers, advertising is increasingly data driven and data responsive. Improved techniques for data collection and analysis increase the ability to be analytical in developing advertising strategies and in evaluating the success or failure of a campaign.

"Imagination and Eloquence," those traditionally valued skills of persuasion, continue to be the most important qualities of an advertising professional, according to the chairman of a worldwide agency. When the person with imagination studies data, he sees a pattern no one else sees, identifies a new trend in the market, or has a flash of insight into consumer behavior. Eloquence persuades, and advertising is in the business of persuasion. Ideas, words, images, color, motion, and music are creatively integrated to produce persuasive messages. That's advertising!

To Explore a Career in Advertising

Read about careers in advertising in comprehensive guidebooks such as *The Harvard Guide to Careers in Mass Media* and the advertising volume of The Career Directory Series. These references will tell you about the many different jobs in advertising, as will chapters in *Choosing a Career in Business*, *Creative Careers*, and *Dream Jobs*. Other publications, like the advertising chapter in *Inside Track*, will convey the "atmosphere" of advertising.

Read the journals and newspapers that people in advertising read. Look at *Advertising Age* and *Adweek*. From this professional literature you will learn about current trends and issues in advertising. You'll also learn advertising jargon and begin to talk and think like an insider; you'll know, for example, that a "hot new shop pitching some great creative" is an up-and-coming young agency competing with superior creative campaigns.

Watch ads. Read ads. Analyze the concept, the presentation, and the overall strategy of the ad. Try writing and developing your own ads. Take a product that you are familiar with and design an advertising campaign to increase its sales. Keeping an advertising career notebook will help you to formulate and articulate a personal philosophy of good advertising, something ad agencies will expect you to have.

Begin to research companies. In the *Standard Directory of Advertising Agencies*, also known as the *Agency Red Book*, you will find staff size, annual billings, and lists of clients for each agency. Study the *Standard Directory of Advertisers* to learn which agency has the accounts of your favorite products. Keep in mind, however, that client lists for ad agencies are constantly changing. Trade magazines will give current news on which agencies have just won or lost a new account.

Make appointments to visit and talk with people in advertising at their offices. As discussed earlier, you can identify potential career advisers from friends and family or from among your college's alumni. If you read about someone in advertising that you would like to meet, write or call and ask for an appointment.

Don't ever interview someone in advertising without doing your homework. Remember that advertising is a very public business. The work of an advertising person is published or broadcast, and therefore available for you and the rest of the public to view, ignore, enjoy, or abhor. Check the *Agency Red Book* to learn what accounts a particular individual's agency serves and then study those ads.

When you meet with people in advertising, try to discover the challenge they find in designing marketing strategies. Join them in their search to understand the needs and drives of people, all kinds of people. Share in their excitement in developing new concepts and experimenting with new technologies.

Visiting people in agencies provides a great opportunity to study their work environment. Does it appear exciting? Hectic? Pay attention to *your* reaction.

Assess your strengths and weaknesses. As you explore the field of advertising, do you get the feeling that it suits you? If so, why? You must be able to articulate your strengths and skills, and whether they are better suited to account management, creative services, or research.

Account Management

If you like to coordinate a lot of different activities, motivate a team of specialists to work together, listen to and persuade clients to reach agreement on ideas and strategies, you might thrive as an account manager.

Account managers are in charge of the ad campaign. From the initial contact with the client to the broadcast of the ad, the account manager is responsible for planning the overall strategy, communicating with the client, keeping the members of the team happy and productive, and meeting all deadlines.

Account managers should be liberally educated and media sophisticated. They should be bright, articulate, thorough, decisive, enthusiastic, able to prioritize and juggle many tasks simultaneously, and open to new ideas and innovative solutions.

Account service people are often called upon to mediate between the client and the other departments within the agency. Their ultimate goal is to satisfy the client without compromising the creative efforts of the agency and to produce the best quality product in the least expensive and most rapid way.

Most people start as an intern, account coordinator, or assistant account executive. Some agencies have training programs; others train new hires on the job.

Two aspects of your job hunt are very important: your written materials and your networking. Your resume should provide information in a two-second scan. The graphics must be imaginative and pleasing, but not detract from the message. Your cover letters must be clever, appealing, and short.

You must keep in touch with all the people in account management whom you met during your exploration, and meet as many more as you can. Advertising is a people business. One way to meet people in advertising and to get tuned in to the informal job network is to join the Ad Club in the city in which you want to work.

Creative Services

If you like to write and are good at it, you might want to be a copywriter. If creating messages interests you, if words fascinate you, you might want to write ads, create slogans, articulate concepts.

If you are a design person, like to paint or draw, or are visual, you might like to be an art director. The ideas for an ad may come from anyone, but the development of the concept is the responsibility of the creative staff. To be competitive "full service" agencies, many "shops" have developed design departments to produce brochures, annual reports, company identity (logo, letterhead, etc.), and product packaging. These departments function as design studios and hire graphic designers.

To compete for a job in creative services, you must prepare a "book." This is a collection of ads that you have designed, written, or drawn. Your book should be creative, intriguing, clever, and as professional as you can make it. For advice on how to develop your book, see *How to Put Your Book Together and Get a Job in Advertising* and *How to Get a Job in Advertising*.

Ask people that you have met in advertising to criticize your book. If you join the local Ad Club, you can ask people you meet through the club to review your book and give you suggestions. You should be constantly improving your presentation.

Traffic, Media, and Production

The traffic department is responsible for scheduling and coordinating all the projects moving through the agency. A traffic coordinator must be detail-oriented, have an understanding of the process of creating and producing advertising, and have great interpersonal skills.

The media department plans and purchases different advertising vehicles to meet the client's needs. This could mean outdoor (billboards), broadcast (television and radio), and print (magazines and newspapers). A media coordinator or assistant must be good at research, comfortable with computers and numbers, and have an interest in how different types of advertising reach targeted audiences.

The production department is responsible for hiring vendors and managing budgets to produce a print or broadcast spot based upon the agreed-upon creative. A production assistant or coordinator must be interested in the technical aspects of producing a spot and must enjoy working with numbers and budgets.

In Conclusion

Advertising is a fast-paced, challenging, creative business. It is a business, not studio art or creative writing. It places high value on imagination, intuition, decisiveness, drive, and willingness to take risks.

Getting a job in advertising requires initiative and persistence, a strong competitive spirit, belief in yourself, and the ability to articulate your strengths.

GO SELL YOURSELF!

Banking

The banking industry is being redefined by changes in the legislative and regulatory environment. Through mergers, consolidations, and internal restructuring, financial institutions such as commercial banks, investment banks, brokerage houses, and insurance companies are developing the capability to offer comprehensive financial services to their clients. Competition is keen as these multiservice organizations enter each other's traditional markets with innovative products and services.

Advances in communications technology, financial deregulation, and the volatility of foreign exchange rates have fueled the continued globalization of capital markets. The development of an active market for swapping the currency and interest rate structure of financings has promoted worldwide integration of capital markets. Not only has the volume of transactions increased dramatically, but so has the array of currencies, securities structures, and specialized products available to bankers for optimizing capitalization.

Investment banks often appear in the headlines as the agents for megadeals in which millions or even billions of dollars are exchanged. Accessing the world's major financial markets, international investment banking firms assist clients in raising capital and executing transactions of securities and other instruments. In addition to managing large public and private securities offerings and arranging mergers and acquisitions, investment banks advise clients on a wide range of financial and strategic matters.

Commercial banks are altering their approach to large corporate clients, upgrading their account officers' skills to emphasize financial engineering and the marketing of a broad array of noncredit products. As one commercial banker has stated: "The fact that we know these clients well means we can go far beyond the traditional lending relationship and bring our corporate finance and investment banking skills to the table. We are placing heavy emphasis on investment banking products where returns are high and claims on capital low, and on innovative corporate finance packages, which include lending, but also allow for free income and higher overall returns on customer accounts."

To maximize the profit opportunities in retail banking permitted under deregulation, major banks are opening customer service offices nationwide, and expanding their product lines. Bankers are borrowing the marketing techniques of soft drinks and soaps to sell financial products to consumers. By targeting specific populations, tailoring financial services and products to meet their needs, and advertising with jingles and slogans, retail banking has discovered new profitability.

Exploring Banking

Banking is a service industry which deals in money. Bankers are in the business of taking care of the financial needs of individuals, corporations, nonprofit institutions, and government.

To orient yourself to the world of finance, read the *Wall Street Journal*. Reading the news highlights on the front page and scanning articles of interest will give you the financial news of the day. The *WSJ* will also introduce you to the perspective of the financial community on current events and issues of concern. The Business section of the *New York Times* would also educate you about financial news, but the *WSJ* is the newspaper that everyone in finance reads.

There are many excellent business magazines: *Fortune* and *Forbes* have very informative articles on finance and banking. Some articles will describe a remarkable success or failure in a particular bank; other articles will focus on successful individuals in banking and give you some insight into what they are like.

If your interest in banking increases as you read about it, it's time to go visiting. Through alumni of your college or your friends, identify bank officers whom you can visit. Arrive early for your appointment so you have time to experience the environment. In your conversation, ask the bank officer what he finds rewarding about his work. To learn about the various divisions of a bank, try to visit officers with different responsibilities and in different banks. To experience the reality of banking, try to get a part-time or summer job in a bank.

Your visits will be much more productive if you read some career guides to the banking industry first. Books such as *Choosing a Career in Business, How to Get the Hot Jobs in Business and Finance*, and *Money Jobs!* depict the structure of banking institutions, describe functions and jobs in banking, and introduce you to the vocabulary that bankers use. *The Wall Street Journal Guide to Understanding Money & Markets* will give you a good grounding in the basics of finance.

Getting Started in Banking

With deregulation, the differences between commercial banking and investment banking have become blurred, but certain differentiating characteristics have tended to persist.

Commercial banks have traditionally emphasized relationship banking. They give high priority to developing long-lasting relationships with their customers and building loyalty by taking care of their financial needs over time. In the expansion of their services to include investment banking, the loyalty of longtime clients is central to their strategy. The objective is to understand the unique financial needs of each customer and develop individualized services to meet those needs.

Traditionally, the commercial loan officer was responsible for researching the credit worthiness of corporate customers. Now these loan officers are frequently responsible for researching the corporate client's financial needs and working with appropriate divisions of the bank to design products to meet those needs.

Most commercial banks have management training programs. At some banks there is one training program for all divisions; at others, there are separate training programs for corporate banking, institutional banking, operations, trust, etc. Some training programs require classroom instruction and homework assignments for six to eighteen months; others mix on-the-job training with seminars. Commercial banks value long-term service, just as they value long-term relationships with customers. This does not mean that you sign a lifetime contract when you accept a job at a commercial bank, but you should plan to stay with the bank after the training program for at least the number of months of the training program.

Investment banks engage in both transactional and relationship banking, but the strategy of most investment banks is to focus on packaging the most profitable deal. Their strategy for attracting business is to build their reputation as innovators in capital formation and masterminds of profitable mergers and acquisitions. They concentrate on the current transaction, bringing together the best deal possible.

Investment banks usually do not have training programs. Newly hired financial analysts have a few orientation meetings and then learn by doing, working seventy to ninety hours a week. Financial analysts usually have a two-year contract, after which most go to business school. Only rarely is a financial analyst promoted to associate.

Other Options in Finance

Commercial banks and investments banks are only two types of institutions in the financial services industry. Insurance companies, brokerage houses, credit unions, and savings and loans associations all offer banking services. Investment counseling, mutual funds, and accounting firms also provide related career opportunities, as do the corporate finance departments of corporations.

Education

Why Teach?

I have always loved to show someone a new way to do something, to help another person work through some problem or to explain something to a friend . . . Perhaps that's why I want to be a teacher, because Harvard has taught me so much to teach, and my experiences here have made me feel as if I can teach.

Two high school social studies teachers . . . had a profound influence on me as both friends and role models. I can think of no better way to repay them for the lessons they taught me than to be an educator in their most fatherly, compassionate, socially-aware tradition.

At first glance, my enthusiasm may be interpreted as idealistic, but I cannot emphasize enough that I recognize the frustrations . . . of attempting to teach children, especially teenagers. This reality is often painful to face . . . but it has never dampened my hope that I will learn how to make a difference in how children learn. My experience with inner-city youths has reinforced my belief that education is crucial . . . Teaching would enable me to try to make a difference in the lives of young people.

I see teaching as a job I would like to do for two or three years and then I'd make a decision to go on to further teaching, education or perhaps another occupation . . . such as medicine. I can think of no better way to prepare myself for other occupations than to be a teacher.

I also want to teach for idealistic reasons; as corny as it sounds, teaching seems to me one of the most noble professions and the passing on of knowledge a keystone of society.

> —Excerpts from personal statements of Harvard College students applying for the teacher education program.

Why teach? Because you like to help others learn, because you think that committed teachers can help improve society, because you aspire to be like the one or two teachers who made a difference in your youth, because it seems like an interesting and challenging thing to do for a couple of years.

What's It Like to Be a Teacher?

If you haven't been in a secondary or elementary school classroom since you were a student, ask your favorite teacher or someone else's favorite teacher if you can visit his classroom. It is very different to be in a classroom as an adult visitor; you will find, for one thing, that you identify with the teacher. As you observe the interaction of the teacher and the students and of the students with one another, you will see education taking place at many levels. The teacher is concerned about what the students are learning, how they are learning, and the intellectual and interpersonal skills they are developing. He tries to plan lessons and activities that will stimulate learning and personal development.

It is very possible to plan experiences that provide you with opportunities to try out teaching. During termtime you can volunteer to be a teacher's aide or assistant, or you may work as a tutor for individual students. As you become familiar with the students and with the subject matter, ask if you may teach a small group, or perhaps prepare and lead some lessons for the whole class.

Working as a camp counselor is also good exposure to the responsibilities and rewards of teaching. Instructing students in sports, crafts, or performing arts; planning and leading group activities; and being responsible for group morale and discipline are all closely related to the profession of teaching.

If you decide that you enjoy leading and sharing in the learning process with young people, teaching may be the job for you. Deciding to become a teacher when you graduate from college does not commit you to being a classroom teacher for the rest of your life. After several years of teaching, you may decide that you love teaching and the classroom is just the place for you. Or you may decide that you want to contribute to schools and education, but that you believe your talents will be better utilized in administration, curriculum development, counseling, or research.

If you decide that you do not want to continue in education, you will find that as a teacher you have developed skills that will help you in your next job. To begin with, you have learned to structure a body of knowledge into logical parts that can be taught as lessons. You have learned presentation skills and group leadership skills. You have probably increased your skills of persuasion, and, if you have survived in the classroom, you have learned how to motivate, interest, and discipline a group.

If you decide that you do want to be a teacher, the next step is to decide if you want to teach in public schools or private schools. Public schools require that you meet state certification requirements; most private schools do not require state certification. At some point you will make choices about geographic location, type of community (rural, suburban, or urban), and perhaps specific school or school district.

Teaching in the Public Schools

In the spring of 1983, eight national reports were published that sounded an alarm about the crisis in the public schools. These reports alerted the nation to many danger signals, including a growing shortage of teachers and the low average test scores of would-be teachers. The recommendations made in the reports were many, but there was broad agreement on several issues: the need to recruit talented, committed young people into teaching; the need to increase teacher salaries; and the need to improve working conditions for teachers. Universities and colleges, state legislatures, and local school districts are responding to these calls for action with many new programs.

The program options for meeting state teacher certification requirements have greatly increased. At Harvard, for example, there are three programs: an undergraduate teacher education program, a one-year master's degree program for liberal arts graduates, and a midcareer math and science teacher preparation program. In many states it is now possible to be hired into a teaching position and meet certification requirements by attending after-school seminars. Summer programs have been developed at some colleges and universities. The array of new certification programs and of new scholarship funds for future teachers has expanded rapidly. Because new programs are being initiated all the time, it is best to supplement this information by inquiring at the universities and colleges in your area or at your state department of education.

Teacher certification requirements differ for elementary and secondary schools and from one state to another, but there is reciprocity between many states. You can research the requirements and the policy on reciprocity in the state in which you want to be a teacher in *Requirements for Certification of Teachers, Counselors, Librarians, Administrators for Elementary and Secondary Schools.*

Teaching in Private or Independent Schools

Independent schools, which are private schools governed by a board of trustees and supported by tuition, grants, and endowment, vary greatly in educational philosophy and structure of program. Some are progressive and innovative, some are conservative and traditional; some are large, some are small; some are day schools, some are boarding schools; some are single-sex, some are coeducational. The individuality and diversity among independent schools is one of their most distinctive characteristics.

Independent schools usually expect that teachers will become involved in activities outside the classroom: sponsoring a student activity; advising or leading a performing arts group; coaching a sport. In boarding schools, young teachers usually live in student dormitories and some serve as proctors and advisers. This involvement with students outside the classroom is rewarding in that it provides the opportunity to know students from a more general perspective. Faculty members play a number of roles in relation to students, and there is a strong sense of community.

Most independent-school teachers are liberal arts graduates who participated actively in their colleges and communities. Most schools do not require prior teaching experience because they can provide supervision and guidance to the new teacher. Experience as a camp counselor, youth group leader, teacher's aide, or tutor is valued as evidence of leadership ability and of sincere interest and concern for young people.

The Job Search

As an applicant for teaching jobs, you may want to prepare a dossier if you have access to a service which will maintain a file of your letters of reference and send it to potential employers upon request. Otherwise you will need to prepare your own packet of materials and identify academic and personal references.

Your resume should communicate your breadth of interests and experiences and document your achievements. It should list your academic major and honors; describe your participation in student and community activities, athletics, performing arts, publications, and your work experience; and describe your travel experience and foreign language fluency, if any. You may need more than one page in order to include all the information that a principal or headmaster might want to know about you.

To make clear the subjects that you are prepared to teach, it is best to prepare an informal transcript that lists your courses by subject area, with descriptive titles.

Most teaching jobs are listed in professional newsletters, in career office bulletins, and in newspapers. You should watch job listings carefully and apply immediately. At the same time, it is wise to identify school districts where you would like to teach and write to the superintendents, enclosing your resume and attachments. The *Directory of Public School Systems in the U.S.* provides useful information about school systems and lists the names of the superintendents.

There are three avenues to teaching jobs in private schools: job listings, direct contact with selected schools, and placement agencies. Attending the annual conference of the National Association of Independent Schools in late February is an efficient way to make yourself available for interviews. Many headmasters attend the convention in order to interview applicants. In recent years increasing numbers of independent schools have paid placement agencies to recruit and interview their teachers. When you register with a placement agency, make certain that you will not be charged a fee.

Private Independent Schools and *The Handbook of Private Schools* will enable you to research the academic programs and extracurricular activities offered at schools to which you might be applying.

Other Starting Jobs in Education

Teaching is the core function in education, and, therefore, experience as a classroom teacher is valued as a foundation for any other career in education. It is, however, possible for a new college graduate to get an excellent introduction to educational administration in positions such as admissions officer, administrative assistant, development assistant, or research assistant in secondary schools or colleges.

Careers in Education

To progress in any career in education, it is important to undertake appropriate graduate study at some time. There are many career paths: school administration, teacher training, curriculum development, educational counseling, and research and teaching in professional schools of education.

Government and Politics

> *Ask not what your country can do for you; ask what you can do for your country.*
>   —John F. Kennedy, January 20, 1961

There are many ways to serve your country, your state, your community, but elected officials and government employees are the people with the direct responsibility for protecting and promoting the public good.

From building more livable cities to protecting the environment, from ensuring equal opportunity to stabilizing and strengthening the economy, from avoiding nuclear war to promoting international economic development, the health and well-being of the people and the nation depend on the skills, the expertise, and the dedication of public officials.

The federal government employs almost three million people, half of whom are college graduates. Many government positions require graduate degrees. There is an incredible variety of jobs ranging from Curator of Early American Painting at the Smithsonian to Field Examiner for the National Labor Relations Board, to Biologist with the Environmental Protection Agency, Social Science Analyst in the Department of Health and Human Services, Language and Country Specialist for Voice of America, and Archaeologist in the Department of Interior.

Federal positions have detailed job descriptions and Civil Service ratings. The compensation structure is designed to give equal pay for equal work. When you take into consideration the Civil Service benefits and job security, the salary schedules are equitable with most of the private sector. Although you won't get rich in government service, career development opportunities with good income potential do exist in some agencies.

State and local governments employ almost five times as many people as the federal government. Approximately half of these are employed as teachers and administrators in public education.

Service to your country, your state, or your community as a public official may be a long-term career commitment or a short-term commitment at any stage of your career. Experience in the public sector can be highly relevant to career development in the private sector; conversely, experience in the private sector is respected and sometimes preferred in competing for positions in the public sector.

Researching Opportunities in the Public Sector

Issue-oriented or expertise-oriented? Two different ways to approach your exploration of government and government-related jobs are by the area of public policy on which you would like to work or by the skills and knowledge that you would like to develop. Either approach will lead you in many directions and increase your knowledge of public sector opportunities. Why not choose the approach that suits your motivation? *The Harvard Guide to Careers in Government and Politics* will launch you in your exploration.

Issue-Oriented Search. If you want to work to protect the environment, focus your research on learning about the departments and agencies of the federal government, the committees of Congress, and the private, nonprofit groups which are concerned with environmental issues. Many agencies of the government in addition to the Environmental Protection Agency (EPA) address environmental issues including: the Council on Environmental Quality, the National Oceanic and Atmospheric Administration in the Department of Commerce, the Department of the Interior, the Land and Natural Resources Division in the Department of Justice, the Division of Policy Research and Analysis in the National Science Foundation, and the Public Health Service.

In Congress, several committees of the House and of the Senate have jurisdiction over legislation on environmental affairs. The General Accounting Office has an Environmental Coordinator who is responsible for auditing and evaluating the programs of the EPA. These governmental agencies and Congressional committee staffs have differing responsibilities including data collection, data analysis, report writing, policy formulation, legislative development, program administration, and program evaluation. Job opportunities within these agencies are many and varied.

Public interest agencies also have many types of jobs for people who want to work on protecting the environment. The programs of each of these private nonprofit agencies differ, but their objectives include educating the public, educating government administrators and legislators, gathering data and writing reports, designing and administering research projects, preparing and conducting litigation, and consulting with the government or with private groups about environmental problems.

There are many areas of public policy that may be of particular interest to you: civil rights, equal opportunity, housing, arms control, child advocacy, hunger and poverty, international cultural exchange, health care. There are government and nongovernment agencies that work in each of these areas.

An excellent reference for an issue-oriented search is the *Washington Information Directory*, which is arranged by subjects such as health, international affairs, law, and justice. Each chapter is subdivided into public policy areas, and in each section there are entries under three categories: departments and agencies of the executive branch of the federal government, committees of Congress, and nongovernmental organizations. After identifying agencies of interest to you in this directory, you will want to turn to other resources such as *Washington 90, The United States Government Manual*, and *Public Interest Profiles* to gain more complete descriptions of what each agency does and to identify the names of officers or administrators.

The limitation of these references is that they focus on the federal government and/or Washington, D.C. Information about other areas of the country and about state and local government can be found in the *Federal Regional Executive Directory*, the *State Executive Directory*, the *Municipal Executive Directory*, and the *State Municipal League Directory*.

Expertise-Oriented Search. If you are fluent in one or more foreign languages, you may decide to focus your research on opportunities to use your language skills. Many departments in the government need language specialists to translate and interpret materials from English into a foreign language or from a foreign language into English. Translations range in difficulty from simple correspondence to complex legal and scientific reports or political negotiations. Individuals who, in addition to language fluency, are knowledgeable about the history, culture, and economy of a country and region, especially at the M.A. or Ph.D. level, are employed in the Department of State and other agencies that deal with foreign countries.

There are also many nongovernmental organizations that need foreign language and culture specialists.

Similarly, if you are a scientist or a social scientist at the B.A. or Ph.D. level, there are opportunities for you in government or government-related agencies. To begin learning about jobs that require special expertise, you might start with the *Dictionary of Occupational Titles*, *Occupational Outlook Handbook*, and the *Federal Career Directory*.

If you have general skills in research, writing, people management, or administration, almost any agency or office may have positions for you. Many young people like to start on Capitol Hill on the staffs of congressional representatives or on committee staffs in order to learn about the legislative process and be involved in politics. Similar positions are available with state legislatures. Another starting place for people with general skills is with nongovernmental agencies: public interest groups, professional and trade associations, and consulting firms. The job market is competitive in all these areas, but interesting jobs do exist.

Job Hunting in the Public Sector

The government job market is highly structured and many jobs require compliance with an exacting job application procedure. It is important to become well informed about the appropriate process for the types of jobs that interest you. Most government jobs are publicly listed, so checking job listings regularly is important. Taking the initiative, however, and making contact with the directors of agencies for whom you would like to work can be beneficial. The *Federal Career Directory* gives contact information for the federal agencies and departments which are part of the competitive Civil Service. It also identifies excepted service agencies (non-Civil Service) and tells how to get employment information from them directly.

If you are a Ph.D. looking for a job that requires your academic background, you should conduct a thorough search to identify all governmental and nongovernmental agencies that might possibly need your expertise. Learn all you can about the activities and projects of each agency. References that would be helpful in this research include professional and academic journals and research reports published by the government or by the agencies themselves.

If you are an undergraduate and would like to work for the government after you graduate, getting related experience through part-time or summer internships is important. If there are particular areas of public policy that interest you, try to arrange academic courses and research projects that enable you to develop some special knowledge in that area. The more related experience you have prior to graduation, the better your chances of securing the full-time position of your choice.

If politics is your interest, get involved. Become politically active in your community and volunteer to work on political campaigns. Look for opportunities to work as an intern for an elected official. Research the employment options working with and for politicians and get to know the career history of politicians you admire. If you are interested in elective office, plan ahead and plan alternatives.

High Tech

What is "high tech"? To most of us it is computers—hardware and software—and that is what will be discussed in this chapter. Actually, the high tech segment includes many industries on the frontiers of technology: biotechnology, telecommunications, aerospace and defense electronics, semiconductors, optics, robotics. All these industries need experts in the hard sciences. They also need experts in finance, marketing, communications, and management.

The computer industry is a fast-paced, rapidly changing business in which products have an average half-life of one year. Innovation, technology-driven and customer-driven, is essential for survival. New products must meet the demands of increasingly sophisticated end-users. Computer capability is addicting: the more users can do, the more they want to do. Product development must be guided by anticipating what customers will need to enhance their productivity.

Computers are a growth industry. Layoffs are episodic, related to unanticipated changes in the market or in the competition from new products. Overall, the industry continues to expand. Each year thousands of start-ups on venture capital seek to turn the corner on profitability by finding the right niche for their product. Creative marketing must be coupled with production capability, which can respond quickly to an increase in demand. Some start-ups will be spectacular successes; most will fail. The marketing objective is to establish the product or products as the de facto standard with which other manufacturers strive to be compatible.

Broadening the base for revenues through diversification is a strategic necessity for maintaining profitability. Product innovation is usually given first priority. Research focuses on the development of new products and new applications for current products. Good customer service translates into more than direct assistance on request. To build product loyalty, corporations are taking the initiative in educating individual and corporate customers through courses, newsletters, and magazines.

Exploring the World of Bits and Bytes, Add-Ons, and Peripherals

You don't have to be a technical whiz kid to be successful in the computer industry, but you do have to be excited about the world of computers. Outstanding technical talents are needed in development and production, but for each technical job there are many nontechnical jobs in writing, human resource management, finance and administration, user education, and corporate communications.

Are you interested in computers, in what it is possible to do with computers, in the technical breakthroughs that are just around the corner? Are you comfortable using a computer? Have you done any programming? How's your computer vocabulary? Do you know the difference between ROM and RAM, floppies and hard disks, spreadsheet and database? Have you taken any courses in computers, or have you spent time on a computer exploring its capacity to perform functions that you need to accomplish?

A great deal has been written about the computer industry. You might want to start with *The High-Tech Career Book* or the VGM Professional Careers Series. Because developments happen so quickly, many of the exciting stories about successful start-ups, new products, and innovative marketing strategies are related in magazine stories. *Fortune, Forbes, Business Week,* and *Inc.* have regular features about the computer industry. There are computer journals and magazines for the technical expert and for the lay user. If you are just starting your research, try *Computerworld.* If you are interested in a particular computer specialty, such as systems design, *Computer Design* and *Electronics* will be interesting to you.

Follow up your reading with visits to people who work in the computer industry. You can identify career advisers from among alumni of your college, friends of friends, or people that you read about in the news. Try to observe and learn about as many different job categories in the industry as possible. What is your reaction to the people you meet, the environment in which they work, and the feelings they express about their work?

One of the decisions you will face is whether to work for a small start-up company or a large established company. In a start-up, you will have varied and changing responsibilities and a fast-moving, risky environment. If the company is successful, the financial rewards may be great. If the company fails, you will be unemployed; but if you have performed your job effectively, it is usually not difficult to get another job. The advantages of a big company are good training programs, better job security, and more predictable career opportunities.

If You Want a Technical Job

If you are a computer science major or have become technically knowledge-able on your own and you want a job in the development or production of hardware or software, the career research outlined above is too elementary for you. You need to research trends in the industry, identify where the state-of-the-art research is being done, study specific products and specific companies. See the section in Chapter 3 on researching employers, keeping in mind that you can apply this advice to your more specialized job search.

You may have a fairly specific focus, based on problems or possibilities that you have become interested in during your academic training. As you review the technical literature related to your research interests, take note of the names of the people and the companies or research facilities where the projects that interest you are taking place. These are the people and employers to contact during your job hunt.

There are many more jobs in software development than in hardware. Software engineers, or computer programmers, write code for new software products or adapt existing programs for specific users. If you do not know how to write computer programs, but you want to learn, apply for a programming training course at an insurance company or bank. Because there is a shortage of programmers, these large employers pay you while you are in training. As your programming skills increase with experience, you will want to be sure you are in an environment that challenges your creativity. If you decide to stay in software development, there are three career pathways: you may focus on your technical expertise and become a guru in a specialized area; you may become a manager of other programmers and advance in technical management; you may move laterally into marketing or finance and become a general manager.

Your resume for a technical job application should list the relevant courses that you have completed and the computer languages in which you are proficient, and describe explicitly your experience in research and development. Using technical language is appropriate because it is more concise and precise and will be understood by your readers.

The work environment for technical personnel varies from one company to another. You will want to know the people you will be working with most closely, the level of support for taking chances, and the expectations of management.

If You Want a Nontechnical Job

Whether or not you have a technical background, you may want a nontechnical job. Computer companies need people who are good problem solvers and can be productive in many different business functions. As one leading software company has stated, "While the range of job categories is broad, including highly technical areas as well as a wide variety of marketing and communication functions, successful candidates will have this in common—the talent and drive to be the best at what they do."

The high tech employer differs very little from employers in other industries. He wants to hire the best possible candidate for the position he is staffing, be it in marketing, management, finance, or communications. The way for you to convince him that you are the ideal choice is to be diligent in your research and presentation. If you do your homework, then you are likely to succeed. Chapters 3 and 4, which describe the job-hunting process, will be especially relevant for you as you begin to identify the entry-level jobs in high tech. If you read *The High-Tech Career Book* and *High-Tech Jobs for Non-Tech Grads*, you will begin to discover the enormous range of possible applications for your particular skills and interests.

Looking Into the Future

Any attempt to flowchart all of the career development possibilities in the computer industry, let alone in the entire high tech universe, would result in an almost limitless number of possible pathways. New technologies will bring new job titles and new industries. Regardless of what they may be, tomorrow's jobs will still require the diversity of technical and nontechnical skills that those of today demand. Success in accessing these positions will depend upon:

1. Your sophistication in researching new ways to use your skills and build on your work experience, your capacity to process the information you gain from industry publications, other media, and your professional network.

2. Your flexibility—your willingness to return to a formal education or training program or to switch modes from technical to nontechnical, or some combination of these two.

3. Your motivation—your drive to be in a "cutting edge" industry or occupation, which is what "high tech" is really all about!

Management Consulting

Consulting is project work, usually fast-paced with specific objectives and deadlines. It is targeted problem solving. The consultant gathers information from interviews, records, and reports, and must make recommendations within a given time frame. Consultants work collaboratively in a team, identifying the questions, reviewing the information when it has been gathered, and sharing insights and ideas. Most of the work—the collection of information, the analysis of data, the writing of reports—is accomplished by individuals working by themselves and is then reviewed by other team members.

People in consulting are bright, articulate, competitive, and hardworking. They travel, meet with top executives, conduct investigations, and prepare reports. They are challenged by the variety of both the types of problems and the types of organizations for which they work.

The job of the consultant is not over when the report is prepared. Persuading executives to implement the recommendations is an integral part of the consulting process. Developing the rapport with the client and earning his confidence during the research phase of the project lays the groundwork for positive reception of the recommendations. In management consulting, the objective is to improve the client's profitability and performance. Success is measured by the way the clients outperform their competitors in earnings and increased market share.

The major portion of management consulting is done in large firms which have hundreds or thousands of employees and offices in major cities around the world. However, consulting may be done by an individual or a very small team. Consulting firms may be highly specialized in the expertise they offer or they may be generalists. There are consulting firms which specialize in contracts from government or nonprofit institutions. Their expertise may not be in any aspect of management, but in a technical or scientific discipline.

Research

Any reading that describes a problem situation in business and the decisions made to try to bring about positive change introduces you to the kind of problem solving that management consultants do. In fact, *In Search of Excellence* is an example of one kind of research that consultants conduct. Written by two consultants, this book analyzes selected corporations and draws conclusions based on that analysis.

The "Consulting" chapter in *Dream Jobs* and the "Business Consulting" chapter in *Choosing a Career in Business* offer synopses of the field, describing the practice of consulting as an individual or as a member of a general or specialized firm. Periodicals such as *Consultants News* or the *Journal of Management Consulting* will further immerse you in the profession.

Most management consulting firms have three tiers: research assistants, associates, and partners. College graduates are hired as research assistants to do research and analyze data, usually for a two-year term. How much the research assistant participates in the gathering of information at the client site, is consulted in the development of the report, or assists in the presentation of the report varies from firm to firm. Very few of the large firms promote research assistants to associates. In most firms the research assistant job is an intense two years of experience studying a variety of industries and corporations. Ordinarily, to be considered for an associate position, an individual must have a graduate degree, usually an M.B.A. Those with a Ph.D. who are hired by large consulting firms usually start as associates, but may have to undertake some special training to learn financial and market analysis. This discussion will focus on entry-level opportunities in large management consulting firms.

Action

Utilize the *Consultants and Consulting Organizations Directory* and the *Harvard Business School Career Guide: Management Consulting* to identify firms that interest you. Read whatever you can find about these firms, in brochures, newspapers, magazines, and journals. Talk to consultants. Listen to their descriptions of the structure of their organizations and their perceptions of their competitors. Ask them about typical assignments for research assistants. Target the firms for which you would like to work.

Implementation

Contact your targeted employers, making a concerted effort to ensure that your presentation is flawless. Your resume must be well organized and efficient. Your cover letter is your primary means of demonstrating your communication skills, your creativity, and your analytic abilities—after all, you must convince the reader that your unique combination of experience and skills is precisely what he needs.

Follow up on your initial contact within the time you specified in your letter; this will indicate your ability to meet deadlines. During your interviews with the firm, remember that your communication and interpersonal skills are being evaluated, along with the other abilities you are presenting. While your responses to questions should not be long and rambling, neither should they be flat and monosyllabic. Think of your interviewer as a client with whom you are attempting to establish some basis for a continuing and productive relationship. A pertinent, well-timed question from you can guarantee that you leave the interviewer with the impression that you are both inquisitive and perceptive, highly desirable traits in consulting.

Conclusion

As stated earlier, an M.B.A. is usually required for promotion to the associate level within a firm; even so, the research assistant position is an excellent way to gain business expertise in a project-oriented environment. An alert and conscientious research assistant can learn much that will be of value in a variety of industries, as well as in nonprofit, public, and education institutions.

Public Service

Public service offers a combination of challenges and satisfactions that are unmatched in any other type of work. In an amazing variety of positions, you can have the opportunity to select the social problem that you feel is most important (unfortunately, there is no lack of candidates) and tackle it head on. You will have a chance to "make a difference," to learn about yourself, to meet people you never knew existed, to work with supportive colleagues, and, with a little luck, make a living at the same time.

What sorts of opportunities exist in public service? They differ in almost every particular.

The type of organization you work with, if you work with an organization at all, may be governmental or nongovernmental, established, or of your own making. Many of the best-known volunteer programs for recent graduates, including WorldTeach, Teach for America, and the Overseas Development Network, were themselves *started* by recent graduates.

On a day-to-day basis, you may help people meet their daily needs for food and shelter, participate in the delivery of health care services and health education, work in education as a teacher or an administrator, or help people prepare for and find employment. Or you may devote your efforts to working for social change as an advocate, organizer, administrator, writer, researcher, or fundraiser.

Public service organizations work on almost any issue imaginable—from public health to lighthouse preservation—and often work on the same issue from two or more opposing sides. Some of the best-known organizations are devoted to social concerns like hunger, poverty, housing, child care, equal employment, civil rights, human rights, public education, and environmental protection.

Public service opportunities can take you to large cities or small villages anywhere in the world. Recent college graduates have taught school in Kenya, run after-school programs in a public housing project, worked in Cambodian refugee camps in Thailand, and helped provide legal services to migrant workers in Maryland.

And "other" interests—such as music, art, sports, business, or science—can be combined with a public service opportunity in ways that you might not have imagined. Sports programs that help inner-city kids, arts opportunities for the handicapped, scientific associations for the promotion of human rights are all important parts of the public service landscape.

Many opportunities in public service are volunteer positions. In foreign countries, this usually means that room and board will be provided. In the Peace Corps, for example, a stipend is paid to cover expenses, and at the end of your contract, you will receive a grant to help you finance your transition period. In this country, most people working in public service agencies begin as unpaid interns, taking part-time paid work elsewhere to help meet expenses. With experience they are able to move into a paid position in the same or a different organization.

There are many opportunities in public service to assume significant responsibility and to gain widely applicable skills in a relatively short period of time. Most agencies are small, loosely structured, and understaffed. They welcome the energetic and thoughtful person who is willing to take on additional responsibilities. It is also possible to create a project of your own to address a social need. Finding a source of funding may be difficult, but it is not impossible. Funding sources tend to respond positively to the creative young public service entrepreneur.

Learning by Doing

You can learn about the rewards and satisfactions of public service by volunteering wherever your assistance is needed. If you live in a city, you can help staff a homeless shelter, become a home visitor to the elderly, or sign up to be a big brother or big sister to a child in need of companionship. If you live in a small community, efforts to assist the needy may be less organized, but reaching out to be a good neighbor to those in need will reap rewards to both them and you. There are many different ways to become involved.

If working on social and political issues is your preference, there are usually groups where you can work to defend or promote the position in which you believe. In a social action group, many routine jobs must be done: sending out large mailings, handing out leaflets at shopping centers, doing door-to-door canvassing, as well as more interesting responsibilities such as writing press releases, doing research to gather supportive documentation, writing and designing brochures. The satisfaction in social action work is not derived primarily from the job functions, which are sometimes mundane, but from the rewards of working with people with whom you share a common commitment.

If you are interested in a particular type of service or in working with a specific population or social issue, the directories listed in the bibliography at the end of Chapter 3 will help you locate agencies in different fields. Because public service work is interdisciplinary, looking at directories in your field of interest can be helpful as you try to focus on what you would like to do. The "Internships and Summer Work" section of the bibliography at the end of this chapter lists internships available in different areas. If you would like to get involved, but have no specific goals, use these directories to learn about what is available.

When you apply for opportunities in public service, your resume and letter should describe your related experiences and activities and make clear your commitment to the objectives of the organization. As stated above, shared motivation toward common objectives is a fundamental aspect of any public service agency. Be sure to specify whether you are able to work without pay. Most organizations rely heavily on volunteer workers. If you have very little experience, that may be the appropriate role in which to start. Keep in mind that volunteers receive priority consideration when paid positions become available.

Vocation or Avocation

Many careers in public service, though by no means all, require professional training. The best way to determine whether advanced study would be most useful to you is to get your feet wet in the field and develop for yourself an idea of what additional skills you need. There are many examples. If you want to help provide health care services to the disadvantaged, you need to become a doctor, a nurse, or a physician's assistant. If you want to help the emotionally disturbed, you will want to train to be a psychiatrist, a clinical psychologist, or a social worker. If you want to help improve urban public schools, you will want to take teacher training and earn state certification. After teaching for a few years, you might take graduate courses to prepare to become a principal or reading specialist or curriculum specialist. If you want to work in legal aid, you will need a law degree. If you want to be a manager in public service agencies or government, you might study for an

M.B.A., an M.P.P., or an M.P.H. Some kind of management and public policy graduate degree may be important in helping you qualify for increased responsibility. In international public service agencies, professional credentials are especially important. *Careers for Dreamers and Doers: A Guide to Management Careers in the Nonprofit Sector* devotes an entire chapter to the education and training of managers for nonprofit organizations.

You may decide that your contributions in public service will be avocational. As former Harvard President Derek Bok has stated: "Whether you will become a lawyer, a doctor, a businessman, or a public servant, you can shape your professional work, your community life, or your private hours to include substantial effort in behalf of others who need your help. If you are to gain real personal fulfillment, your responsibilities to others must be planned for, worked for, incorporated into your lives."

SOURCES

Career Descriptive Literature

The Academic's Handbook. A. Leigh Deneef, Craufurd D. Goodwin, Ellen Stern McCrate, editors. Duke University Press, Durham, NC, 1988.
> Essays grouped by topic: the academy and the academic; academic employment; teaching and advising; funding academic research; publishing research; academic administrations. Brief bibliography. Indexed.

The American Almanac of Jobs and Salaries. John W. Wright. Avon, New York, NY, 1987.
> Examines various positions in the public, private, and nonprofit sectors, with salary information taken from Department of Labor and Department of Commerce data.

Architect? A Candid Guide to the Profession. Roger K. Lewis. MIT, Cambridge, MA, 1985.
> Examines the architectural field from a number of perspectives. Discusses education and practice, pointing out the satisfactions and frustrations encountered along the way. Lists accredited architecture programs.

Becoming an Environmental Professional 1990: Articles from Leading Environmental Professionals on Employment and Career Trends in the 1990s—Plus Proceedings from the CEIP Fund's Sixth Annual Environmental Careers Conference "What on Earth Can You Do?" The CEIP Fund, Inc., Boston, MA, annual.

Aimed at both first-time job seekers and career changers, as well as those already in the field. Resource list.

The Career Directory Series. The Career Press, Inc., Hawthorne, NJ, 1989/90.

Eight Volumes: *Advertising, Book Publishing, Business and Finance, Magazine Publishing, Marketing and Sales, Newspapers, Public Relations,* and *Travel and Hospitality.* Each guide is packed with information about the field and ideas for getting started, including lists of potential employers, internships, and sources of further information.

Career Opportunities for Writers. Rosemary Guiley. Facts on File Publications, New York, NY, 1985.

Describes 91 jobs in eight major fields, with salary and career development information. Appendixes list: educational institutions; professional, industry, and trade associations and unions; major trade periodicals; bibliography. Job title index.

Career Opportunities in Aging: A Handbook for the Future Professional in Gerontology. Cecile P. Strugnell. University Center on Aging, University of Massachusetts Medical Center, Worcester, MA, 1983.

Examines the various career fields which offer the opportunity to work with older people. A good introductory section on gerontology career planning and job-search strategies. Selected bibliography.

Career Opportunities in Art. Susan H. Haubenstock and David Joselit. Facts on File Publications, New York, NY, 1988.

Describes 75 different positions in the field, with salary and career development information. Appendixes list schools, funding opportunities, professional organizations, and resources. Job title index.

Career Opportunities in Television, Cable, and Video. Maxine K. Reed and Robert M. Reed. Facts on File Publications, New York, NY, 1986.

Describes 100 jobs in the field, with salary and career development information. Excellent bibliography.

Career Opportunities in the Music Industry. Shelly Field. Facts on File Publications, New York, NY, 1986.

Provides salary, skill requirement, career path, and other information for 79 jobs in the performing, business, and educational areas of the music field. Appendixes list educational programs, organizations, etc., including a glossary. Indexed.

Career Preparation and Opportunities in International Law. John W. Williams, editor. Section of International Law and Practice, American Bar Association and International Law Institute, Washington, DC, 1984.

Describes international legal career opportunities in the public, private, and nonprofit sectors, with information on the specific preparation needed in each case.

Careers for Dreamers and Doers: A Guide to Management Careers in the Nonprofit Sector. Lilly Cohen and Dennis R. Young. The Foundation Center, New York, NY, 1989.

Describes employment opportunities, includes career profiles, and provides job-hunting tips. Includes a list of associations involved in career advancement and professional development, as well as a United Way summary of position classifications and foundation position definitions. Bibliography. Indexed.

Careers in Information. Jane F. Spivack. Knowledge Industry Publications, Inc., White Plains, NY, 1982.

Explores entry into the "information" field from a variety of backgrounds: computer science, library science, information science, management and accounting, engineering, communications, and journalism. A good introduction to a career field particularly hospitable to liberal arts and arts and sciences graduates.

Careers in International Affairs. Linda L. Powers, editor. School of Foreign Service, Georgetown University, Washington, DC, 1985.

An introduction to international work in a variety of settings, including business, education, government, nonprofits, research, and international organizations. Identifies and describes potential employers and provides addresses. Bibliography. Index.

Careers in Marketing. David W. Rosenthall and Michael A. Powell. Prentice-Hall, Inc., Englewood Cliffs, NJ, 1984.

Profiles 26 career categories within the marketing field, including nonprofit marketing. Includes alternate job titles, position requirements, comments from individuals in each field, bibliographies. Index of job titles.

Careers in Mental Health: A Guide to Helping Occupations: The Opportunities in Mental Health and How to Prepare for Them. Paul Schmolling, Jr., William R. Burger, and Merrill Youkeles. Garrett Park Press, Garrett Park, MD, 1986.

Provides an overview, along with descriptions of specific mental health careers and work settings. Includes a chapter on self-assessment. Lists resources.

Careers in Sports. Jack Clary. Contemporary Books, Inc., Chicago, IL, 1982.

Identifies a range of sports-related occupations, including such areas as sports management and industrial recreation.

Careers in the Nonprofit Sector: Doing Well by Doing Good. Terry W. McAdam. The Taft Group, Washington, DC, 1986.

Describes the sector and the job-search process, including the decision to accept or reject an offer. Includes case studies and sources of additional information.

Catalyst Career Opportunity Series. Catalyst, New York, NY, 1987.

Forty briefs and two career planning booklets with information about different occupations. Each career brief is divided into two sections. The first provides an in-depth and candid look at an occupation by profiling an individual in a specific job; the second gives "fast facts" about the industry in general, including the salary level and the education and training needed to enter the field. The two career planning booklets give an overview of the process of career planning.

Choosing a Career in Business. Stephen A. Stumpf and Celeste Kennon Rodgers. Simon & Schuster, New York, NY, 1984.

Examines the required skills and background for various business careers; describes each field and relevant job functions. Includes a chapter on job-hunting strategy. Bibliography.

Choosing a Career in the Law. Dena O. Rakoff. Office of Career Services, Harvard University, Cambridge, MA, 1991.

Gives an overview of the profession, describes the law school application process and curriculum, and introduces some law-related fields. Lists additional sources of information.

The Complete Guide to Environmental Careers. The CEIP Fund. Island Press, Washington, DC, 1989.

Provides an overview of the field, as well as chapters on specific areas of interest within the field. Includes interviews with professionals, job-search strategies, salary information, internship and volunteer ideas, and resource lists. Indexed.

Corporate PhD: Making the Grade in Business. Carol Groneman and Robert N. Lear. Facts on File, New York, NY, 1985.

Profiles of Ph.D.'s who pursued careers in the private sector, and interviews with employers who have hired Ph.D.'s. Stresses the transferability of skills from the academic to the corporate world.

Creative Careers: Real Jobs in Glamour Fields. Gary Blake and Robert W. Bly. John Wiley & Sons, Inc., New York, NY, 1985.

An introduction to advertising, book publishing, finance, gourmet food, movies, music, photography, television, the theater, travel, and tourism. Includes resources and glossaries.

Dictionary of Occupational Titles. 4th edition, U.S. Department of Labor, U.S. Employment Service, U.S. Government Printing Office, Washington, DC, 1977.

Contains almost 17,500 job titles and their definitions, arranged by type of occupation. A good way to get an overview of the different job possibilities within a given field, although not all will be of interest to the liberal arts graduate. Occupational title and industry indexes. DOT Supplement published in 1982; includes many high tech titles.

Dream Jobs: A Guide to Tomorrow's Top Careers. Robert W. Bly and Gary Blake. John Wiley & Sons, Inc., New York, NY, 1983.

An introduction to advertising, biotechnology, cable TV, computers, consulting, public relations, telecommunications, training and development, and travel. Includes resources and glossaries.

Federal Career Directory. United States Office of Personnel Management. Superintendent of Documents, U.S. Government Printing Office, Washington, DC, 1990.

Describes federal career and employment opportunities, including internship and student employment programs.

For Fun and Profit: Self-Employment Opportunities in Recreation, Sports and Travel. Live Oak Publications, Boulder, CO, 1984.

Examines self-employment opportunities in the recreation field, including physical fitness, sporting goods, etc. Appendix lists additional sources of information, including books, periodicals, and associations.

Foreign Languages and Your Career, 3rd edition. Edward Bourgoin. Columbia Languages Services, Washington, DC, 1984.

Introduces the various career fields in which foreign language skills are important or necessary. Lists additional sources of information, including organizations. Index of occupations.

Getting into Fashion: A Career Guide. Melissa Sones. Ballantine Books, New York, NY, 1984.

Profiles jobs in the apparel, retail, and textile industries. Includes interviews with professionals in the field, and has a separate chapter on getting the first job. Lists educational programs and additional sources of information.

Getting into Film, revised edition. Mel London. Ballantine Books, New York, NY, 1985.

Provides an overview of the industry and describes jobs in the field. Lists unions and training programs; has chapters on grants, festivals, job hunting, etc.

Guide to Cruise Ship Jobs. George Reilly. Pilot Books, Babylon, NY, 1989.
Describes the jobs available and gives job-hunting tips. Lists major cruise lines and firms that recruit for cruise ship companies. Basic nautical glossary.

Guide to Federal Jobs. Rod W. Durgin, editor-in-chief. Resource Directories, Toledo, OH, 1985.
Profiles government agencies, includes selected job descriptions, and describes the application process. College major and job category indexes are helpful, but by no means comprehensive; they are a good place to start, though. One appendix lists Federal Job Information Centers.

The Harvard College Guide to Investment Banking. Marc Cosentino. Office of Career Services, Faculty of Arts and Sciences, Harvard University, Cambridge, MA, 1990.
Chapters on corporate finance, public finance, sales and trading, entry-level positions, and retail brokerage. Includes four appendixes: dilemmas and decisions, internships, sample resumes, and a reading list. Glossary.

The Harvard Guide to Careers in Government and Politics. Lynn Bracken Wehnes. Office of Career Services, Faculty of Arts and Sciences, Harvard University, Cambridge, MA, 1991.
A beginner's manual for those contemplating employment in government and politics, with references to additional sources of information for the job seeker. Has a particular emphasis on working in Washington, Foreign Service careers, and campaign work.

The Harvard Guide to Careers in Mass Media. John H. Noble. Office of Career Services, Harvard University, Cambridge, MA, distributed by Bob Adams, Inc., Holbrook, MA, 1989.
Profiles eight career fields within the entertainment media, news media, publishing, and promotional media. Includes annotated bibliographic references, case studies, and job-hunting tips.

The Harvard Guide to Consulting. Marc P. Cosentino. Office of Career Services, Faculty of Arts and Sciences, Harvard University, Cambridge, MA, 1991.
An introductory chapter on consulting in general, followed by essays on the specialties within the field, each written by an expert practitioner.

Health Career Planning: A Realistic Guide. Ellen Lederman. Human Sciences Press, Inc., New York, NY, 1988.
Focusing on the allied health fields, this book opens with a chapter on the decision-making process, then proceeds to a discussion of the student years, first years on the job, career development, stress on the job, and career change. Indexed.

The High-Tech Career Book: Finding Your Place in Today's Job Market. Betsy A. Collard. Crisp Publications, Inc., Los Altos, CA, 1986.

An excellent guide to the high tech field. Examines types of organizations, as well as functional areas (engineering, marketing, sales, writing, public relations). Gives practical advice on the job-search process and profiles industries and trends. Resource list, glossary, index. Packs a lot of information into one volume!

High-Tech Jobs for Non-Tech Grads. Mark O'Brien. Prentice Hall, Inc., Englewood Cliffs, NJ, 1986.

Strategies for identifying and gaining nontechnical employment in high tech companies. Includes brief sketches of some high tech fields and some case studies.

Jobs in Arts and Media Management: What They Are and How to Get One! Stephen Langley and Jamers Abruzzo. ACA Books, New York, NY, 1990.

Describes the various career fields and offers job-hunting advice. Lists graduate programs in arts administration, arts and media management internships, seminars, workshops, information centers, referral services, membership associations, and periodicals with job listings.

Jobs '90. Kathryn and Ross Petras. Prentice Hall Press, New York, NY, 1990.

Contains career outlooks by field, industry forecasts, and a regional profile of employment prospects. Lists additional sources of information, as well as major employers by industry and state. Special reports on women, minorities, and disabled workers.

Lawyers in Transition: Planning a Life in the Law. Mark Byers, Don Samuelson, and Gordon Williamson. The Barkley Co., Inc., Boston, MA, 1988.

Describes ways in which lawyers can develop their careers both within the law and in alternative professions. Contains chapters on self-assessment and the job search, as well as an annotated bibliography.

Market Wizards: Interviews with Top Traders. Jack D. Schwager. New York Institute of Finance, New York, NY, 1989.

Includes traders from a variety of backgrounds and environments, with a chapter on the psychology of trading. Appendixes on program trading and portfolio insurance and options. Glossary.

Nonlegal Career for Lawyers in the Private Sector, 2nd edition. Frances Utley with Gary A. Munneke. American Bar Association, Chicago, IL, 1984.

Examines career possibilities in business, educational foundation, service, and other organizations, with job-hunting tips. Resource section.

Occupational Outlook Handbook. U.S. Department of Labor, Bureau of Labor Statistics, Government Printing Office, Washington, DC, biennial.

Describes in detail about 250 occupations. Keyed numerically to the *Dictionary of Occupational Titles*, this book describes the nature of the work conditions, training, employment outlook, earnings, and related occupations. Lists sources of additional information.

Occupational Outlook Quarterly. U.S. Department of Labor, Bureau of Labor Statistics, Occupational Outlook Service, Washington, DC, quarterly.

Contains articles on new occupations, training opportunities, salary trends, career counseling programs, etc.

Paralegal: An Insider's Guide to the Fastest-Growing Occupation of the 1990s. Barbara Bernardo. Peterson's Guides, Princeton, NJ, 1990.

Describes the field; includes listings of professional associations and training programs. Bibliography.

Planning Your Medical Career: Traditional and Alternative Opportunities. T. Donald Rueker and Martin D. Keller. Garrett Park Press, Garrett Park, MD, 1986.

Aimed primarily at college juniors considering medical school, this book provides an overview of the profession and the health care delivery system. Describes medical specialties, as well as nonclinical roles for physicians. Lists resources. Indexed.

Practicing Law in New York City. James J. Fishman and Anthony S. Kaufmann, editors. Council of New York Law Associates, New York, NY, 1975.

Describes various specialities with the law, and examines different settings for their practice. Includes sections on minorities, volunteer public service work, and interviewing for a position.

Profitable Careers in Nonprofit. William Lewis and Carol Milano. John Wiley & Sons, Inc., New York, NY, 1987.

Profiles positions within the nonprofit area and discusses the job-search process. Lists resources and professional associations. Indexed.

Requirements for Certification of Teachers, Counselors, Librarians, Administrators for Elementary and Secondary Schools. John Tryneski. The University of Chicago Press, Chicago, IL, annual.

Geographically arranged. The appendix lists addresses of state offices of certification.

TV Careers Behind the Screen. Jane Blanksteen and Avi Odeni. John Wiley & Sons, Inc., New York, NY, 1987.

Describes the television industry and jobs relating to the production of television programs. Includes interviews with people working in television production. Resource lists. Indexed.

VGM Opportunities Series. VGM Career Books, Lincolnwood, IL.
> More than 100 titles, each examining a career field and providing basic information on positions and required qualifications. Many provide sources of additional information.

VGM Professional Careers Series. VGM Career Books, Lincolnwood, IL.
> Separate volumes examine careers in accounting, business, communications, computing, education, engineering, health care, and science. A good way to gain an overview of the various positions and career paths within each field.

The Wall Street Journal Guide to Understanding Money & Markets. Richard Saul Wurman, Alan Siegel, and Kenneth M. Morris. Access Press Ltd., New York, NY, 1989.
> Explains stocks, bonds, mutual funds, futures, money supply, etc., in easily understood language, complete with illustrations, charts, graphs, and tables. Indexed.

Directories of Career Literature and Counselors

Books in Print. R.R. Bowker Co., New York, NY, annual. Updated by Books in Print Supplement.
> *Books in Print,* the basic source of information concerning books offered for sale by distributors and publishers in the United States, includes author and title listings. There is a separate, subject-classified *Subject Guide to Books in Print,* where career-relevant publications are listed under Library of Congress subject headings. This resource can be found in most bookstores, as well as in library reference collections.

Directories in Print. Julie E. Towell & Charles B. Montney, editors. Gale Research, Inc., Detroit, MI, bienniel.
> An invaluable annotated guide to about 10,000 directories published in the U.S. and Canada. Arranged in 16 major subject categories. Includes computer-readable formats. Title/keyword and subject indexes.

Directory of Counseling Services. Nancy E. Roncketti, editor. International Association of Counseling Services, Alexandria, VA, annual.
> Listing of the association's member organizations in the U.S. and Canada, including those at colleges and universities.

National Directory of Career Resource Centers. Catalyst, New York, NY, no date.
> This pamphlet geographically lists centers that provide career development services and programs, including three international listings; includes a Catalyst publications list. Updated by a two-sheet supplement in March 1990.

Directories of Trade and Professional Journals and Associations

Encyclopedia of Associations. Gale Research, Inc., Detroit, MI, annual.
Volume 1 provides details on active nonprofit organizations of national scope, arranged in 18 subject categories, with name and keyword index. Volume 2 is a geographic and executive index to Volume 1. Volume 3 supplements Volume 1. A companion volume, International Organizations, describes international nonprofit membership organizations (including national organizations based outside of the U.S.), and includes geographic, executive, and name and keyword indexes.

Gale Directory of Publications and Broadcast Media. Gale Research, Inc., Detroit, MI, annual.
Geographically lists media, including trade journals, radio and television stations, and cable systems in the U.S., Puerto Rico, and Canada, with cross-reference indexes for specific types of publications and radio station format. Includes names, addresses, and telephone numbers of newspaper feature editors. Master name and keyword index.

Hudson's Subscription Newsletter Directory. Margaret Leonard, editor. Hudson's Newsletter Directory, Rhinebeck, NY, 1990.
Selective listings of subscription newsletters in the U.S. and abroad, by subject and geographic location. A separate section contains information of interest to someone in or considering entering the newsletter trade. Title index.

National Trade and Professional Associations of the United States. Columbia Books, Inc., Washington, DC, annual.
Lists trade and professional associations and labor unions with national memberships. Subject, geographic, budget, and acronym indexes.

Standard Periodical Directory. Oxbridge Communications, Inc., New York, NY, annual.
A comprehensive directory of U.S. and Canadian periodicals, including trade journals, newsletters, house organs, yearbooks, etc. "Periodical," in this case, refers to any publication issued at least once every two years. Although some of the descriptions are quite sketchy, this is a good place to get some basic information on obscure publications. Title and subject indexes.

Ulrich's International Periodicals Directory. R.R. Bowker Co., New York, NY, annual, with quarterly updates. 3 volumes.
A subject listing of over 111,000 periodicals from around the world. A particularly helpful feature is the "Subject Guide to Abstracting and Indexing." This will lead to publications which index the periodicals in a particular field. Index to publications of international organizations, title index.

Internships and Summer Work

Directory of Financial Aids for Minorities. Gail Ann Schlachter. Reference Service Press, San Carlos, CA, biennial.
Lists "scholarships, fellowships, loans, grants, awards, and internships designed primarily or exclusively for minorities." Annotated bibliography. Program title, sponsoring organization, geographic, subject, and calendar indexes.

Directory of Financial Aids for Women. Gail Ann Schlachter. Reference Service Press, San Carlos, CA, biennial.
Lists "scholarships, fellowships, loans, grants, awards, and internships designed primarily or exclusively for women." Annotated bibliography. Program title, sponsoring organization, geographic, subject, and calendar indexes.

Farm, Ranch and Country Vacations. Pat Dickerman. Farm and Ranch Vacations, Inc., New York, NY, 1986.
Geographic listing of farms, ranches, lodges, and inns, with a separate chapter on country vacations abroad. Appendix identifies ranches with cattle drives, places that can accommodate one's horse, and those involved in organic gardening. Indexed.

Getting Work Experience: The Student's Directory of Professional Internship Programs. Betsy Bauer. Dell, New York, NY, 1985.
Arranged by career field, with an introductory chapter on internships and what to expect from them. Index of companies and organizations, geographic index.

Goodworks: A Guide to Social Change Careers. 3rd edition. Joan Anzalone, editor. Dembner Books, New York, NY, 1985.
Information on 600 social change groups and internship and volunteer opportunities with them. Profiles on individuals in the field and additional sources of information. Geographic and topical indexes.

Internships: 50,000 On-the-Job Training Opportunities for Students and Adults. Brian C. Rushing, editor. Peterson's Guides, Princeton, NJ, annual.
Includes international listings and introductory information on internships. Separate section lists Washington, D.C. opportunities. Bibliography. Geographic and sponsor indexes.

Jobs in Paradise: The Definitive Guide to Exotic Jobs Everywhere. Jeffrey Maltzman. Harper & Row, New York, NY, 1990.
Lists jobs in the U.S., Canada, the South Pacific, and the Caribbean by category: high adventure, mountains, tropical islands, snow & skiing, coasts & beaches, rivers, lakes, deserts, tour escorts, amusement & theme parks, cruise ships, and miscellaneous. Alphabetical and geographic employer indexes.

National Directory of Arts Internships. Warren Christensen, editor. National Network for Artist Placement, Los Angeles, CA, biennial.

> Listings in all areas of the arts. Good introductory section on developing an internship, with practical advice on cover letters, resumes, portfolios, etc.

The National Directory of Internships. Amy S. Butterworth and Sally A. Migliore, editors. National Society for Internships and Experiential Education, Raleigh, NC, 1989.

> Internships and fellowships arranged by type of organization. Alphabetical, geographic, and field indexes.

National Parks Trade Journal, 3rd edition. Robert Frankel, editor. Taverly Churchill Publishing, Yosemite National Park, CA, 1989.

> Introductory information on working in National Parks and at resorts, followed by geographically arranged listings of seasonal and career positions, articles, and interviews. Includes international opportunities.

New Careers: A Directory of Jobs and Internships in Technology and Society. Rachel Helfand, editor. Student Pugwash USA, Washington, DC, 1990.

> Contains advice for interns, bibliography, and a separate section on jobs and internships with the government. Geographical and issue area indexes.

Peterson's Summer Opportunities for Kids and Teenagers. Peterson's Guides, Princeton, NJ, annual.

> Lists programs geographically, with a separate section of two-page descriptions for some programs. Includes international listings, a quick-reference chart of basic information, and a number of specialized indexes (special needs, religious affiliations, financial assistance, etc.). Many of the programs listed regularly hire college students to work for them. Alphabetical index of programs.

The Student Guide to Mass Media Internships. Ronald H. Claxton. Intern Research Group, Department of Journalism, Southwest Texas State University, San Marcos, TX, annual.

> Newspaper, magazine, public relations, and broadcasting internships. Within each category, annotated listings arranged alphabetically by state and city. Gives deadlines and contacts.

Summer Employment Directory of the United States. Pat Beusterien, editor. Peterson's Guides, Princeton, NJ, annual.

> Geographically arranged job listings, mostly at resorts, ranches, restaurants, lodgings, summer theaters, summer camps, and national parks, although some business and government listings. Most listings include the name of a contact person, salary information, and any fringe benefits. Includes a few foreign listings and an introductory section on the summer job hunt.

Summer Opportunities in Marine and Environmental Sciences. Joy A. Herriott and Betty G. Herrin. White Pond Press, Londonderry, NH, 1985.

The subtitle, "A Compilation of Jobs, Internships, Study Camp and Travel Programs," sums up the scope. Brief bibliography.

Summer Theatre Directory. Jill Charles, compiler and editor. American Theatre Works, Inc., Dorset, VT, annual.

Geographically arranged listings of theaters, theme parks, and summer training programs, some in Canada. Tips on auditioning and finding the "right" summer theater apprenticeship, internship, and employment information for performers, directors, designers, technicians, and managers. Alphabetical index of theaters.

Taking Off: Extraordinary Ways to Spend Your First Year Out of College. Lauren Tarshis. Fireside, New York, NY, 1989.

Lists paid and volunteer opportunities abroad, volunteer opportunities in the U.S., and paid opportunities in the outdoors in the U.S. Lists resources.

Work and Study Abroad

Academic Year Abroad. E. Marguerite Howard, editor. Institute of International Education, New York, NY, annual.

Information on over 1800 postsecondary study programs that take place in other countries during the academic year. Geographic listings include deadline, credit, and cost information. Sponsoring institution, field of study, and academic level and special option indexes.

Access to the World: A Travel Guide for the Handicapped. Louise Weiss. Henry Holt and Co., New York, NY, 1986.

Provides information on the policies, services, and accessibility of major airlines, bus lines, railroads, cruise lines, and hotel chains. Lists some independently operated hotels, as well as tour operators, travel agents, and travel organizations. Separate chapters on travel health and additional travel tips. Indexed.

Adventure Holidays. Victoria Pybus, editor. Vacation-Work, Oxford, England, distributed by Peterson's Guides, Inc., Princeton, NJ, annual.

For those who want a focus to their travels, this book is a good place to look. Programs are listed geographically within each activity; features pursuits such as cycle touring and gorilla tracking. Index of companies and organizations.

Alternatives to the Peace Corps: Gaining Third World Experience. Institute for Food and Development Policy, San Francisco, CA, 1990.
>Introductory information, followed by listings of international and U.S. voluntary service organizations, study tours, and alternative travel groups. Resource lists. Index of organizations.

The Au Pair and Nanny's Guide to Working Abroad. Susan Griffith and Sharon Legg. Vacation Work, Oxford, England, distributed by Writer's Digest Books, Cincinnati, OH, 1989.
>Describes the work, the process of securing a position, and what kinds of problems to expect. Includes a country by country guide and a directory of agencies (with contacts). Appendixes on safety, childhood ailments, cooking, and play.

Central America and the Caribbean - Development Assistance Abroad: A TAICH Regional Directory of U.S. Nonprofit Organizations in Overseas Development Assistance. Technical Assistance Information Clearing House of the American Council of Voluntary Agencies for Foreign Service, Inc., New York, NY, 1983.
>Alphabetical listing of U.S. development organizations, followed by a geographic listing of programs in the region. Country, program, and organization indexes.

China Bound: A Guide to Academic Life and Work in the PRC. Karen Turner-Gottschang with Linda A. Reed. National Academy Press, Washington, DC, 1987.
>Written for the Committee on Scholarly Communication with the People's Republic of China, this book discusses practical issues from passports and visas to quality of life once there. Resource lists. Indexed.

Commonwealth Universities Yearbook. The Association of Commonwealth Universities, London, England, annual.
>Geographically arranged information on Commonwealth institutions. Institution and topic, field of study, and name indexes.

Current Research in Britain. The British Library. West Yorkshire, England. Separate annual volumes for physical sciences, biological sciences, and social sciences; biennial humanities volume.
>Lists research in progress by institution. Name, study area, and keyword indexes.

Directory of American Firms Operating in Foreign Countries, 11th edition. World Trade Academy Press. Uniworld Business Publications, New York, NY, 1987. 3 volumes.

> Volume One contains alphabetical listings of U.S. firms operating overseas providing, in some cases, names of president/CEO, chief foreign officer, and personnel director. Volumes Two and Three index firms by country, and include name and U.S. address of parent firm as well as name and address of subsidiary or affiliate in that country.

Directory of Foreign Firms Operating in the United States, 6th edition. World Trade Academy Press. Uniworld Business Publications, Inc., New York, NY, 1989.

> Firms grouped by country, listing their American affiliates. Foreign firm and American affiliate indexes.

Directory of Overseas Summer Jobs. David Woodworth, editor. Vacation-Work, Oxford, England, distributed by Writer's Digest Books, Cincinnati, OH, annual.

> Geographic arrangement of summer employment opportunities; includes volunteer work. Visa, residence, and work regulation information.

Directory of U.S. Based Agencies Involved in International Health. National Council for International Health, Washington, DC, 1988.

> Alphabetical listing of organizations. Lists contacts. Classifies organizations by country and activity.

East Africa—Development Assistance Abroad: A TAICH Regional Directory of U.S. Nonprofit Organizations in Overseas Development Assistance. Technical Assistance Information Clearing House of the American Council of Voluntary Agencies for Foreign Service, Inc., New York, NY, 1984.

> Alphabetical listing of U.S. development organizations, followed by geographic listing of programs in the region. Country, program, and organization indexes.

Emplois D'Ete en France. VAC-JOB, Paris, France. annual.

> Organized both geographically and by type of job. Chapters on au pair arrangements, boarding and lodging, and information for foreign students. In French.

European Technical Consultancies. Daphne M. Tomlinson, consultant editor. Longman, Harlow, England, 1989.

> Lists consulting firms by country (for Western Europe). Companies and acronyms, services, industries served, and personal name indexes.

Fellowships, Scholarships, and Related Opportunities in International Education. Center for International Education, University of Tennessee, Knoxville, TN, 1986.

> Alphabetically arranged; aimed at U.S. citizens and permanent residents. Area of study index.

Financial Aid for Research, Study, Travel, and Other Activities Abroad. Gail Ann Schlachter and R. David Weber. Reference Service Press, San Carlos, CA, biennial.
> Lists scholarships, fellowships, loans, grants, awards, and internships for high school/undergraduate students, graduate students, postdocs, and professionals/other individuals. Annotated bibliography. Program, sponsoring organization, geographic, subject, and deadline indexes.

Financial Resources for International Study: A Definitive Guide to Organizations Offering Awards for Overseas Study. The Institute of International Education. Peterson's Guides, Princeton, NJ, 1989.
> Alphabetically arranged by sponsor, with sponsoring institutions, fields of study, and academic level indexes. Introductory chapter on planning international study.

Ford's Freighter Travel Guide . . . and waterways of the world. Ford's Travel Guides, Northridge, CA, semiannual.
> Arranged by port or waterway, lists schedules and itineraries of freighters that carry passengers. Includes listings of travel agents and foreign government tourist offices. Index of steamship lines.

Ford's International Cruise Guide. Ford's Travel Guides, Northridge, CA, quarterly.
> Complete schedules for over 100 cruise ships. Cruise ship and cruise line indexes.

Funding for Research, Study, and Travel: Latin America and the Caribbean. Karen Cantrell and Denise Wallen, editors. Oryx Press, Phoenix, AZ, 1987.
> Alphabetically arranged by sponsor, with subject and sponsor type indexes. Annotated bibliography includes online databases.

Funding for Research, Study and Travel: The People's Republic of China. Denise Wallen and Karen Cantrell, editors. Oryx Press, Phoenix, AZ, 1987.
> Alphabetically arranged by sponsor, with subject and sponsor type indexes. Annotated bibliography includes online databases.

The Harvard Guide to International Experience. William G. Klingelhofer. Office of Career Services, Harvard University, Cambridge, MA, 1989.
> Chapters on preparing to go abroad, study abroad, work abroad, volunteering abroad, and funding the international experience, each with its own bibliography.

Higher Education in the European Community: Student Handbook, 6th edition. Brigitte Mohr, editor. Oryx Press, Phoenix, AZ, 1990.
> Published by the Commission of the European Communities, this directory provides information on courses, institutions, requirements, fees, funding, etc., for the twelve member countries. Includes resource lists and glossaries.

Higher Education in the United Kingdom. The Association of Commonwealth Universities. Longman, Inc., New York, NY, biennial.

> Arranged by subject, with information on overseas students, money matters, entry to the U.K., student life, etc. Lists sources of additional information.

The International Corporate 1000: A Directory of Those Who Manage the World's Leading 1000 Corporations. Monitor Publishing Co., New York, NY, annual.

> Company listings by region; parent company, subsidiary, division and affiliate, geographical, industry, and individual's name indexes. Time zone and world holiday charts.

International Jobs: Where They Are, How to Get Them: A Handbook for Over 500 Career Opportunities Around the World, 3rd edition. Eric Kocher. Addison-Wesley Publishing Co., Reading, MA, 1989.

> Part one, "International Career Planning and Job Strategy," covers the process of getting a job. Part two, "The International Job Market," profiles employers across a range of fields, from the federal government through teaching and international law. Bibliography. Index.

International Research Centers Directory. Darren L. Smith, editor. Gale Research Inc., Detroit, MI, biennial.

> Multinational section, followed by listings by country. Name and keyword, country, and subject indexes.

The International Schools Directory. European Council of International Schools, Inc., Petersfield, England, distributed by Peterson's Guides, Inc., Princeton, NJ, annual.

> Profiles member schools geographically. Separate sections for affiliate and supporting member schools. Geographic index gives statistical information on international schools worldwide, including non-ECIS schools. Separate indexes of schools offering boarding facilities and the international baccalaureate.

Invest Yourself: A Catalogue of Volunteer Opportunities. Susan G. Angus, editorial coordinator. Commission on Voluntary Service and Action, New York, NY, 1984.

> Alphabetical listings of agencies, with indexes indicating summer and international/intercultural opportunities, as well as work camps and categories of skills and interests needed.

The ISS Directory of Overseas Schools. International Schools Services, Princeton, NJ, annual.

> Geographically arranged profiles of American-style primary and secondary schools. Indexes of schools offering the international baccalaureate and schools with boarding facilities. Lists accrediting associations and regional and international organizations. Indexed.

Japanese Colleges and Universities 1989: A Guide to Institutions of Higher Education in Japan. The Association of International Education, Japan. Maruzen Co., Ltd., Tokyo, Japan, 1989.

Sponsored by Monbusho (The Ministry of Education, Science and Culture), this book describes institutions for the benefit of foreign students. Includes information on scholarships, Japanese language programs, and study abroad programs. Majors and institution indexes.

The Job Hunter's Guide to Japan. Terra Brockman. Kodansha International, New York, NY, 1990.

A brief overview, followed by field-by-field descriptions of opportunities and the job-hunting process. Includes a chapter on corporate culture and an appendix with visa information, listings of professional/support organizations and companies that hire foreigners, and a bibliography.

Jobs in Japan. John Wharton. Global Press, Denver, CO, 1988.

A combination how-to and where-to survival guide. Listings of private English schools.

Kibbutz Volunteer. John Bedford; revised by Deborah Hunter. Vacation-Work, Oxford, England 1986.

Introductory chapters on life in Israel, kibbutzim, moshavim, and other work opportunities. Contains an alphabetical listing of kibbutzim, and application information.

Let's Go Travel Guides. St. Martin's Press, New York, NY, annual.

Budget travel guides, researched and written by students for Harvard Student Agencies, these volumes provide good, practical travel advice and ideas for exploration of various geographic locales.

Looking for Employment in Foreign Countries. 8th edition. June L. Aulick, editor. World Trade Academy Press Inc., New York, NY, 1990.

General information on working abroad in a variety of settings, followed by brief country profiles. Chapters on resumes and cover letters and interviewing. Indexed.

Opportunities to Serve through Canadian and International Organizations. Canadian Conference of Catholic Bishops Missions Office, Ottawa, Ontario, no date.

Includes contacts and application and remuneration information. Subject index. In English and French.

Overseas Development Network Opportunities Catalog. Stanford International Development Organization, Overseas Development Network, Stanford, CA, 1985.

Guide to internships, research, and employment with development organizations. Alphabetically arranged; includes contacts. Geographic index.

The Overseas List: Opportunities for Living and Working in Developing Countries.
David M. Beckmann et al., Augsburg Publishing House, Minneapolis, MN, 1985.
Examines employment in the Third World, from public service opportunities
to those in the private sector; includes a chapter on study and tourism; lists
resources throughout. Activities, geographic, and organization indexes.

Schools Abroad of Interest to Americans. Donna Vierra and Heather Lane, editors.
Porter Sargent Publishers, Inc., Boston, MA, 1988.
Geographic listing of elementary and secondary schools. Includes some postsecondary schools, specialized opportunities, and summer sessions. Alphabetical index to schools.

*Staying Healthy in Asia, Africa, and Latin America: Your Complete Health Guide
to Traveling and Living in Less-Developed Regions of the World.* Dirk G. Schroeder.
Volunteers in Asia, Inc., Stanford, CA, 1988.
Discusses prevention, diagnosis, and treatment of illnesses and first-aid emer-
gencies. Indexed.

Study Abroad. UNESCO, Paris, France, triennial.
Describes international study programs offered by institutions in 126 countries, with section devoted to financial assistance. International organization,
institution, subject of study indexes. In English, French, and Spanish.

Study in the United Kingdom. Edrice Howard, editor. Institute of International
Education, New York, NY, annual.
Provides information on study programs in Great Britain and Ireland. Spon-
soring institution and field of study indexes.

Summer Jobs Britain. Emily Hatchwell, editor. Vacation Work, Oxford, England,
distributed by Peterson's Guides, Princeton, NJ, annual.
Arranged geographically and topically; includes volunteer work.

Survival Kit for Overseas Living for Americans Planning to Live and Work Abroad,
2nd edition. L. Robert Kohls. Intercultural Press, Inc., Yarmouth, ME, 1984.
Includes an examination of culture and values. Resource list.

U.S. Nonprofit Organizations in Development Assistance Abroad, 8th edition,
Technical Assistance Information Clearing House of the American Council of
Voluntary Agencies for Foreign Service, New York, NY, 1983.
Describes, in some detail, nearly 500 U.S. organizations involved in develop-
ment work in the Third World. Category, country, organization, and state
indexes.

Vacation Study Abroad. E. Marguerite Howard, editor. Institute of International Education, New York, NY, annual.

Provides information on over 1300 study abroad programs that run from late spring to early fall. Lists both U.S.- and foreign-sponsored programs. Geographic listings include deadline, credit, and cost information. Sponsoring institution and field of study indexes.

Vagabond Globetrotting: State of the Art, revised edition. M.L. Endicott. Enchiridion International, Cullowhee, NC, 1989.

Travel information arranged by topic (money, health, food, etc.). Annotated bibliography.

Volunteer! The Comprehensive Guide to Voluntary Service in the U.S. and Abroad 1990-1991 edition. Adrienne Downey, editor. Council on International Educational Exchange and Commission on Voluntary Service and Action, New York, NY, 1990.

Basic information on voluntary service followed by short-term and medium/long-term project listings. Organization/publication, skills, and program location indexes.

Work, Study, Travel Abroad: The Whole World Handbook. Del Franz, editor. Council on International Educational Exchange. St. Martin's Press, New York, NY, biennial.

This publication is packed with information and advice on work and study abroad, with numerous references to other sources of information. A good place to start researching an adventure. Indexed.

Work Your Way Around the World. Susan Griffith. Vacation Work, Oxford, England, distributed by Writer's Digest Books, Cincinnati, OH, 1989.

Introductory information on work and travel, with advice and suggestions. Sections on different types of work, as well as geographic listing of employment opportunities.

Working Holidays. Central Bureau, London, England, distributed by Institute of International Education, New York, NY, annual.

Geographically arranged work and volunteer opportunities. Written for the reader in the U.K., but still helpful for North American readers. Index of organizations.

World Chamber of Commerce Directory. Loveland, CO, annual.

Lists chambers of commerce geographically. Includes state boards of tourism, convention and visitors bureaus, and economic development organizations in the U.S., as well as American chambers of commerce abroad, foreign tourist information bureaus, and foreign chambers of commerce in the U.S. A separate section provides listings for the U.S. Congress, dean of diplomatic corps, foreign embassies in the U.S., and U.S. embassies.

The World of Learning. Europa Publications Limited, London, England, annual.
Geographic arrangement of educational institutions, libraries, learned societies, and scientific and cultural organizations. Separate section on international organizations. Index of institutions.

Worldwide Government Directory with International Organizations. Cambridge Information Group Directories, Inc., Gaithersburg, MD, annual.
Part I is arranged by country and outlines the governmental structure, including the legislative and the judicial, as well as the central bank, UN mission, and major foreign embassies located in the country. Part II lists international organizations alphabetically, including United Nations organizations, agencies, commissions, etc.

Chapter 2

CAREER DECISION MAKING

PREPARING FOR CAREER DECISIONS

Developing Your Own Style

Taking charge of your own career development requires making decisions. There is no one right way to make decisions. Different individuals make their career decisions differently. The balance between rational step-by-step processing of facts, meditative reflection, and intuitive leaps will vary from one person to another, and may change for a particular individual from one decision to the next. When a decision seems important, you may hesitate to trust your intuition. However, because it is not possible to know all the facts about yourself and about career options, intuition may be your best guide.

No matter what your decision-making style, becoming well informed improves the quality of your decisions. Getting to know yourself, your values, your interests, and your abilities helps you identify opportunities that may be exciting to you. Learning about the opportunities in a variety of career fields can help you identify what characteristics are important to you.

Exploring careers through reading, interviewing career advisers, and arranging career-related experiences enables you to learn about a variety of career options and to identify your own priorities and attributes. This knowledge guides your research of opportunities that interest you. Each career decision results from a mix of assessment of the facts available to you, advice from significant others, personal reflection, and your intuitive sense of what is best for you.

Increasing Your Self-Knowledge

Being able to describe your strengths, your preferences, and your goals is fundamental to directing your career development. Becoming aware of and learning to express what your special talents are, what you find exciting, and what you find rewarding is an important component of career decision making.

As you gather career information by visiting career advisers at work and by arranging short-term work experiences, see if you can identify with the people you meet. How are you like them? How are you different? Could you do what they do if you had the appropriate training? Would you enjoy doing what they do? Do you share similar values and goals?

Some people find that vocational interest tests assist them in developing self-knowledge. The information that the particular test analyzes is registered by you as you respond to the items. In the scoring process, the data that you have provided are analyzed to produce an interest profile. Validating this interest profile by checking it against what you have learned from your past experiences can accelerate your development of self-knowledge.

Interest tests also correlate your interest profile with the average profile of people in a variety of occupations. This information can help you to identify some occupations that you might want to explore. From this profile of occupations you can also derive some insight into what job characteristics are important to you.

Some people find self-assessment exercises help them to increase their self-knowledge. Exercises can bring into conscious awareness your preferred activities, interests, and values and give you the opportunity to think about them objectively. *What Color Is Your Parachute?* is one good resource for self-assessment exercises.

Tests and exercises, however, cannot do the work for you. You must learn to be analytical about yourself and to trust your own perception of your strengths, your preferences, and your values.

Keeping Your Options Open

If you do not feel ready to make a commitment that structures your options for the future, such as going to medical school or law school, it is very possible to plan employment that gives you opportunities to work with professionals in the field, to explore your talents, and to discover what you find rewarding.

While you are deliberating about your long-range goals, you may want to take a job that is related to your leading career option, or you may want to arrange an experience that is completely away from your probable career. Sometimes an adventure working abroad for a year or two or exploring an avocational interest helps you to clarify your long-range goals.

LIVING WITH INDECISION

You are living in a society that is very career-oriented. Since you were very young, people have been asking you, "What are you going to be when you grow up?" What was your answer? How did you feel about it? Now that you are "grown-up," how do you answer this question? You may be undecided about your career direction because of a lack of information about yourself and what you want in your career, or because you do not want to make a commitment to a specific career field at this time. Whatever the source of your indecision, you need to accept and learn to live with that indecision. The following are some of the strategies students have developed for living with indecision.

Take a short-term view of your planning. Commit yourself whole-heartedly to your current educational endeavors: be the best English or biology scholar that you can be. Learn as much as you can and develop your reading and writing skills. Make the most of the intellectual and educational resources that you have around you.

Enter into the college community activities. Focus on making the institution a better place, or engage in community work. Help make life a little better for those who are less fortunate than you by serving as a volunteer.

Collect new experiences. Seek interesting and preferably different experiences every summer and every year that you are in college. Live fully in the present. This approach to your college experience will give you information which will help you make informed career choices when you are ready to think about the future.

Another way to live with career indecision is to take on a different career identity each semester or year. When you are trying out a particular career identity, visit people who are in that career, read everything you can find about that career, and arrange work experiences which will bring you into contact with people who are pursuing that career. This will enable you to wear that career label knowledgeably and seriously. When people ask you about your career plans, answer with whatever your tentative career identity is. You will quickly learn what their particular evaluations of that career are. Trying on a different career identity each semester will give you the opportunity to experience how that role feels. It will be an interesting experience and it will broaden your knowledge about career opportunities available to you.

If you are undecided because there are two or three career fields that you would like to develop, explore the possibility of pursuing two careers at one time. Or perhaps you can integrate two fields of work into one career. Rather than forcing yourself to give up one of two alternatives that interest you, explore the possibility of pursuing them sequentially. In this case, you will have to decide which to enter first. It is likely that many of you will participate in more than one career field in your lifetime.

One of the best ways to live with career indecision in this career-oriented society is to begin a planned program of career exploration. Visiting career advisers who themselves experienced long years of indecision can be an affirmation of your current state of mind. Having experiences that prove there are interesting alternatives that you might pursue is also reassuring. As you engage in career exploration, it may be helpful for you to set target dates by which you hope to make a tentative decision about the career in which you plan to work after graduation.

LIVING THROUGH CAREER CHANGE

Changing career fields is a common phenomenon. People no longer believe that they must stay in the same field for their whole lifetime. Some people are even programming a career change long in advance, planning to be in their first career until they are thirty, forty, or fifty, and then moving to a new field.

A change of career field is often stimulating and leads to marked increase in productivity, as well as satisfaction and a sense of self-worth.

Different career fields provide opportunities for different modes of self-expression, different kinds of relationships with people, and different contributions to the community. Changing careers allows you to expand your range of accomplishments, experience new kinds of rewards, and develop new talents.

Sometimes people decide to make a change because their current pursuit is not meeting their expectations. Some of the reasons that cause people to begin thinking about career changes are:

- Desire to learn something new
- Insufficient challenge in the work
- Uncertainty about future career opportunities
- Insufficient reward or satisfaction in the work
- No jobs available in the preferred location
- Lack of values and perspectives in common with colleagues
- Work more demanding or less demanding than expected
- Disappointment in the financial rewards
- Failure to gain admission to graduate or professional school

Only you can weigh the pros and cons of your experience in a particular career field and decide whether the balance is positive or negative. If you are dissatisfied and feel unrewarded, this is a strong indication that you should begin exploring other fields.

Give Yourself Time

When you decide that you want to make a career change, it is usually best not to quit your job or drop out of school. Learning about new careers takes time. It is usually unwise to try to rush this process. The activities and lifestyles of other career options may be very different from those you have been experiencing in your current career. Give yourself time to experiment with these different career identities before you set your new career goals or take a job in a new field.

If you can decrease your responsibilities in your current work, perhaps working part-time instead of full-time, you will be able to devote more time and energy to exploring new career fields.

Translate Your Skills

At first you may have difficulty recognizing how the skills which you have developed in your current career field will be valuable in other career fields. Analyzing the functions that you have been performing and your accomplishments will help you to identify the talents you have been utilizing. Self-assessment exercises are designed to lead you through a self-analysis of skills. You will find several books about self-assessment listed at the end of this chapter. Also, the discussion of work attributes in the section "Presenting Yourself on the Job Market" in Chapter 3 provides questions which will help you to increase your awareness of your general work skills. As you research new career options and learn about the work people do in each field, you will gain new insights and new vocabulary for assessing and translating your skills.

Select New Careers to Explore

Your first task is to analyze your present situation. Why are you considering a change? Why were you attracted to this career field originally? What aspects of the career—its functions, roles, rewards, and environments—do you enjoy, and what aspects of the career make you unhappy? A review of the section on "Career Dimensions" in Chapter 1 may be helpful to you in making this analysis.

If you have identified with this first career for some time, it may be difficult for you to select the three to five alternative careers that you might now explore. It may help to think back to the careers you dreamed of when you were a child. What careers did your teachers or relatives suggest to you? Another source for new ideas about careers may be your avocational activities.

If you have been a member of an organization, what kind of roles and functions have you usually filled in those organizations? Are there potential career opportunities related to any of your avocational interests? A third source of new career ideas would be from vocational interest tests. The *Strong Campbell Interest Inventory* and the *Jackson Vocational Interest Survey* give you feedback on how your particular pattern of interests correlates with the interest profiles of people in a variety of career fields. Look back at the section on "Identifying Careers to Explore" in Chapter 1 for more methods of generating a list of career options.

If you explore only one career alternative, you will cheat yourself. At any turning point, there are many career options for you. If you explore at least three different options, you will have more variables to evaluate. By imagining yourself in at least three different career fields and thinking about how each feels, you will learn more about yourself and have more opportunity to assess what your career priorities are.

Exploring New Career Options

Your best method for learning about new options will be from reading and interviewing. The types of literature that will be helpful to you were described in Chapter 1. Reading is the best way to get started in your exploration because you can fit it into your leisure time.

Interviewing people at work and experiencing the environment in which they work will be an essential part of your career search. It is best to interview both young people who are in their early years in a particular field and established people, in order to gain a variety of perspectives on career opportunities. If you are employed full-time in your current work, you may have to talk with people outside of their working hours, but this will limit the possibilities of getting a feeling for their daily work and environment.

Finding a Career-Change Mentor

Find somebody who will listen to you as you assess the pluses and minuses of the career fields you are exploring and contrast them with your present situation. You are seeking a friend, a spouse, a career counselor: somebody who does not have preconceived notions of what you should be, who will listen to you and ask you questions to help you clarify the feelings that you are having during this career transition. The choice of your new career will be yours alone, but having someone to whom you can relate your experiences, and with whom you can examine reactions to those experiences, can be very supportive and productive.

Although the prospect of making a change may seem difficult to you now, the challenges and opportunities of new responsibilities will add richness and diversity to your life experience.

SOURCES

Career Planning Today, 2nd ed. C. Randall Powell. Kendall/Hunt Publishing Company, Dubuque, IA, 1990.
> A comprehensive look at the process of career planning, from self-assessment to job search to career advancement. The "Guide to Selected Topics" provides a good overview of the material.

Kiplinger's Take Charge of Your Career. Daniel Moreau. Kiplinger Books, Washington, DC, 1990.
> Discusses self-assessment and the job search for the midcareer searcher, with chapters on interviewing, evaluating offers, and fitting in with a new corporate culture. A separate chapter lists the best jobs and places. Indexed.

Kissing the Dragon: The Intelligent Work-Hunter's Companion. Madeleine Pelner Cosman. Bard Hall Press, Tenafly, NJ, 1984.
> Somewhat offbeat guide, aimed at self-assessment for Ph.D.'s who are exploring nonacademic careers. There's probably an idea or two in it for anyone.

Part-Time Professional. Diane S. Rothberg & Barbara Ensor Cook. Acropolis Books Ltd., Washington, DC, 1985.
> Profiles individuals and a limited number of employers in the private sector. Explores part-time employment with government agencies. Discusses relevant issues and strategies for negotiating with employers.

Playing Hardball with Soft Skills: How to Prosper with Non-Technical Skills in a High-Tech World. Steven J. Bennett. Bantam Books, New York, NY, 1986.
> Although aimed primarily at the individual contemplating an entrepreneurial venture, the self-assessment suggestions can benefit anyone. Good bibliography.

Self-Assessment and Career Development. 2nd edition. James G. Clawson et al. Prentice-Hall, Inc., Englewood Cliffs, NJ, 1985.
> Stresses self-assessment in combination with career, job, and lifestyle planning. Excellent appendix of sources of information on selected industries and job and career opportunities. Not a book to be rushed through!

What Color Is Your Parachute? A Practical Manual for Job-Hunters and Career Changers. Richard Nelson Bolles. Ten Speed Press, Berkeley, CA, annual.
> Emphasis on exercises as a means of self-evaluation, with listings of additional sources of information on careers and job hunting. Indexed.

Chapter 3

JOB HUNTING

INTRODUCTION

In deciding what kind of job you will seek, you may give priority to particular work tasks, work styles, work environments, rewards, or social commitment, in any combination or hierarchical order. Knowing the job characteristics that are important to you will help you focus your job hunt, increase your efficiency in researching employers, and improve the tailoring of your presentation.

The next four sections describe the functions of your job hunt. These are not sequential steps, but interdependent, ongoing activities. The questions about which you seek information in your research will become more specific as your job hunt progresses. For each job possibility that you identify, you must research the job, the organization, and the industry or field. The knowledge that you gain from your research will enable you to improve the appropriateness, clarity, and sophistication of your presentation. Checking regularly for job listings will keep you informed about the job market. Continuing to identify employers for whom you would like to work and making contact with them will increase your visibility as a candidate on the job market.

Your job hunt may stretch out for several months, involve contact with hundreds of people, and require research into many organizations. In your career research file, described in Chapter 1, you must keep a record of every contact you make and of the outcome of each contact; copies of every letter sent and received; notes on your interviews, not only the content of the conversation, but also your reactions and observations; and notes on your research. This information should be organized and filed so that it is retrievable. Remember that you are engaged in a project which has an uncertain end point. At any time, because of new information about jobs or about yourself, you might decide to change the direction of your search. At that time, you might need to review the records of your job hunt from a new perspective.

False Assumptions About Job Hunting

1. *Contacts can get you the job.* Wrong. Not in this competitive job market. Contacts can help you by referring you to colleagues. Contacts can help you get an interview for a job, but only you can win yourself a job offer.

2. *You are imposing on an employer when you initiate contact with him to express interest in his organization.* Usually not. Executives are on the lookout for talent to meet their present or future needs. If you have qualifications that an employer values, he will be interested in meeting you. You may become part of his talent pool.

3. *Employers can assess in an interview whether you are the person to do the job.* That depends on you. Employers do not have mystical powers that enable them to divine your suitability to fill their position. You must communicate your qualifications. Employers are experienced in assessing candidates, but it is your responsibility to convey why you feel you are the best candidate to do their job.

4. *Employers will hire the person with the best job skills.* Not always. Employers look for personal qualities as well as job skills. They want a person who will "fit in," who will be productive, who will strive for outstanding performance. Many job skills can be learned on the job, but personal qualities are more difficult to develop or change. Different employers look for different personal qualities, but all employers selecting new employees balance the job skills and personal qualities of candidates.

5. *All job openings are advertised.* Not true. It is estimated that only 10 to 20 percent of job openings are advertised publicly. Many jobs are filled by promoting people from within the organization. Other jobs are filled by the employer's informing his colleagues that he has a job to

fill. If, through your information interviews, you make yourself known on the job market, you may be the person the colleague recommends for his friend's job opening.

RESEARCHING EMPLOYERS

The researching of employers is a continuing process which you begin during your career exploration and which becomes more focused and detailed during your job hunt. The more descriptive and evaluative information about employers and their organizations that you have as you proceed with your job hunt, the better you will be able to tailor your approach to each specific employer.

Employers assume that, if you are interested in their organization, you will take time to learn something about it before your first interview. One reason it is helpful to focus on one or two job objectives is that you can concentrate your research on that industry or field, the organizations within the field, and the entry-level jobs.

Characteristics of the Industry or Profession

The first level of research is to gain background on the industry, field, or profession. You are interested in the history, traditions, impact on society, organizations, products, services, markets, and the expected growth. You are interested in information about current issues and developments and the effect of economic and political trends.

Career literature is similar in structure to the literature in an academic field. There are books that relate the history, describe the leaders, analyze the present condition, and/or give recommendations for the future. There are periodicals and newspapers that give news of current events, discuss issues, report research findings, and describe innovative programs. The section on "Using Career Literature" in Chapter 1 and the bibliography at the end of that chapter will lead you to these publications.

During your job hunt, you should read regularly the magazines, journals, and newspapers that your potential employers read. Learn to view current events from their perspective. Be informed on newsworthy developments relating to their field.

Information About Corporations or Organizations

Before you make contact with a corporate employer, you should have basic information about the company: its products or services, number of employees, location of plants and offices, sales volume, and income and growth record. If it is an educational institution, you want to know its history and traditions, its current programs, its financial status, the demographics of the student body. If it is a job in government that you are applying for, you want information about the place of this department in the organizational structure, its budget stability, its mandate, its recent history. With every type of employer, you want as much information as you can gather about the "corporate culture," the quality of interpersonal relationships, the informal channels of communication, the pride people take in their work, and the kinds of behavior and achievement that are rewarded.

The corporate annual report or other company literature, the college or school catalog, government manuals, and directories will contain this information. There are indexes to periodical literature for all major career fields. Looking up the name of a corporation in the *Business Periodicals Index* or *Predicasts Forecasts* gives you a list of recent journal and newspaper articles about that corporation. The *Current Index to Journals in Education* is the best guide to recent articles about educational institutions. The *Readers Guide to Periodical Literature* or newspaper indexes such as the *Wall Street Journal Index* and the *New York Times Index* are helpful for many career fields.

Description of the Job, Work Environment, and Career Opportunities

When you are an applicant for a particular job, you want to learn about the characteristics of the work, its tasks, its pace, its goals, and its rewards. You want to learn what the opportunities for advancement are, and what the usual pathway and time schedule for promotion is. You also want to learn about the work environment, its human and physical characteristics. Referring back to the "Career Dimensions" section in Chapter 1 may be helpful to you in identifying the questions that you want to be asking about each job for which you apply.

Only limited information of this kind is available in print. Some employers publish job descriptions and career development information about their organizations. Some of the general career literature you have read has descriptions of jobs, organizational structure, career development patterns, and group values, but most of this information you will get from people who are inside the organization and from your own observations.

Other Sources of Information

Information about the kind of people who work in an organization, their collegial relationships, their morale and commitment, the style of supervision and performance evaluation, and the quality of informal and formal communication is learned during interviews. If you are called back for a second interview, you should try to meet with the person who currently has the job in which you are interested, or someone in a similar position. You may also be able to identify people who have recently left the organization and can give you inside information.

Job hunters sometimes fail to think analytically and evaluatively about their personal observations. When you are visiting a potential employer, you have the opportunity to observe many characteristics of the work environment: the physical surroundings, the people, the interpersonal relationships, and the work pace. When you are recording the information which you gained in your interviews, include your impressions, observations, and reactions to being in the work setting. In thinking about the question "Would I be happy in this organization?" give careful attention to the subjective data from your personal observations during your visit.

The well-informed applicant is an attractive applicant. Your research on each employer should continue right up to the time you make a decision about a job offer.

PRESENTING YOURSELF ON THE JOB MARKET

You must make clear to the employer that you have the qualities that he is seeking. By means of your resume and attachments, your cover letter, and your letters of reference (if you decide to send them), you want to communicate to the employer that you are the kind of person who will be a productive and respected worker in his organization.

Often liberal arts graduates and graduate students think employers are looking for specific job-related skills. To some extent and for certain types of jobs, this is true. As you read job listings, you might get the impression that the applicant must have two to five years of directly related experience in order to qualify. In reality, however, for many jobs employers are looking for somebody they will like, who will fit into their organization, and who can readily learn to do the job that needs to be done.

Thinking about the following questions will help you describe work characteristics that you have which employers value.

Do you set high standards for yourself and persevere to achieve your goals? Any evidence of high achievement, such as academic honors, varsity athletics, awards in music or the arts, is a sign that you set high standards and have the discipline to endure long periods of training and practice for deferred gratification. If you are goal-oriented, you will speak in terms of achievements rather than in terms of effort expended or functions performed.

Are you sensitive to others' feelings and cheerful and thoughtful in your interaction with colleagues? Almost all work requires that you relate to other people. Employers look for people whom they enjoy. They look for applicants who will be compatible with colleagues and clients.

Do you have a high level of energy and are you able to channel it into a productive effort? People who lead busy lives engaging in a variety of activities and yet meeting their responsibilities and deadlines are people with high energy levels and self-discipline.

Are you cooperative? Do you take instruction well and work well with others? Experience in working with others on projects and programs or in team sports teaches you to be an effective team member.

Do you have the ability to lead, to organize, and to supervise other people? Leadership experience in any kind of organization provides you with the opportunity to develop leadership skills. Be sure your resume describes the leadership experiences you have had.

Do you take initiative? Do you wait to be instructed before you act or do you act on your own, thinking through new ways to get the job done?

Have you had the experience of losing as well as winning? Are you able to lose and continue to give your best effort? Experience in winning and losing comes most dramatically in athletics, but there are other competitive activities in which you may have won and lost.

Are you curious? Do you seek new adventures? Are you excited about learning new skills and knowledge? Are you excited about assuming new responsibilities and learning to become productive? Starting a new job in a new environment with new people is a risky adventure. If you have had a variety of work or travel experiences, you have learned to adjust to new situations; you have learned to function in unfamiliar circumstances.

Do you have the capacity to be loyal? In your life so far have you committed yourself to people and to organizations? Are you loyal to your friends, to your college, to former employers, to your family, to your hometown? It is not what you have been loyal to, but whether you have the capacity to be loyal which will interest employers. If you are negative and critical about your past jobs and associations, employers fear you might be that way about their organization.

Do you have high expectations of yourself? Do you have high aspirations? Employers ask what you hope to be doing in five or ten years to get an indication of how ambitious you are.

These are all qualities which in varying degrees may be important to an employer as he evaluates candidates for a particular position in his organization. You have probably developed some attributes more than others. In your job hunt you should be prepared to communicate to employers through your written materials and your interviews the work qualities and competencies that you have developed.

You may also have some specific job-related skills which make you attractive to a particular employer. As a liberal arts student or graduate student you have highly trained analytic, research, and communication skills. In the university, where your colleagues are articulate, learn quickly, and reason clearly, you may take these skills for granted. Remember that the employer values the person who is bright, thoughtful, and decisive, and the person who is able to express himself well in writing or in speech.

The following are a few of the job skills which it is possible to acquire through academic courses:

- Accounting
- Bibliographic research
- Computer applications
- Computer programming
- Filmmaking
- Foreign language fluency
- Laboratory research
- Math and statistics
- Writing

If you are interested in a job that requires or prefers specific skills, you may want to learn them before your job hunt. Courses in each of these subjects may be taken as electives, as part of your regular academic program, or in evening, summer school, or correspondence courses. See the "Graduate and Professional Education" section of the bibliography at the end of Chapter 5. Some students prefer to learn on their own subjects such as math, statistics, computer programming, or accounting. *Essentials of Accounting* and books in the Schaum's Outline Series or the Harcourt Brace Jovanovich College Outline Series are programmed texts for self-study which some students have used to learn these job-related skills.

It may be that your field of study either as an undergraduate or as a graduate student will be relevant in your job hunt. For example, specific knowledge in the sciences, in applied math, in economics, in foreign languages, or in regional studies can be relevant to certain jobs in business and government. However, the purpose of this chapter has been to alert you to the general work characteristics which you have been developing during your formal education that are important to employers.

You need to be able to talk about yourself: to describe how you approach work, what kind of tasks you do best, what types of goals you set for yourself, what sorts of interpersonal relationships you handle effectively, and what kinds of roles you usually take in an organization.

Your past experiences and the way in which you describe them, the way in which you talk about your achievements and what you have learned from adventures, will communicate to employers the kind of work attributes you will bring to your next job.

Every career field has its own vocabulary which you will be learning from your reading and from your interviews. In planning your resume, your cover letter, and your interview, you should use the appropriate vocabulary and concepts to describe your past experiences and your work attributes.

USING JOB LISTINGS

Although you should not limit your job search to applying for listed jobs, it is worthwhile to do careful research to identify the best job listings in your field and in your geographic area. Job listings help you learn job titles and descriptions and assess the job market. Even if you do not find any jobs for which you wish to apply, you may generate ideas of kinds of jobs that you would like or identify employers for whom you would like to work.

Career Services on Campus

Most schools have placement or career planning offices which provide a variety of services: job listings from employers seeking recent graduates, newsletters with a sampling of the jobs listed in the office, an on-campus recruiting program, a career reference library.

If you participate in on-campus recruiting, you should make your choices with care. If you are not interested in a company, do not waste your time and that of the recruiter by signing up "just for the experience." This will not do either of you any good, and it will deprive another student of a valuable opportunity.

You should not rely solely on on-campus recruiting for a job after graduation. On-campus recruiters represent only a small sample of the employers who might be interested in hiring you. In addition, you may be more successful in securing an interview when you contact an organization on your own; your letter and resume may receive a closer reading than if they were part of a large shipment!

Newspaper Want Ads

The largest listings of local want ads will be found in the Sunday edition of a city newspaper such as the *Boston Globe* or the *Los Angeles Times*. You will find three kinds of want ads: those placed by employment agencies, listing the types of jobs that they have available; large want ads from large corporations; and very small want ads from small employers. You are quite likely to find the more interesting entry-level jobs in the brief listings in small type.

Want ads in local or suburban papers are sometimes the best way to learn about jobs in small organizations. It is less expensive to advertise in the local papers, and sometimes small employers prefer to reach only the audience to which the local paper is distributed. If you do a comprehensive review of newspaper want ad sections and job listings as you begin your job hunt, you can assess which papers you want to continue to review regularly.

Jobs Listed by Institutions

Most universities, hospitals, and other large institutions publish job listings on a regular basis. Large employers have a personnel office, and there is usually a place in the personnel office where jobs are posted. If you are hoping to find a job with a particular employer, it is usually worthwhile to visit the personnel office to see what kinds of jobs are listed there and to make personal contact with someone in the office.

Where to Find Job Listings in Your Career Field

Most career fields have trade and professional journals or newspapers in which there are job listings. For example, social service and community organization jobs are listed in the monthly newspaper *Community Jobs*; jobs in the performing arts are listed in *ArtSEARCH*, published twenty-three times a year; *National Business Employment Weekly* reprints the collected job listings from four regional editions of the *Wall Street Journal*.

The Standard Periodical Directory can lead you to job listings; it has an "Employment" heading that lists, in addition to many others, the three periodicals cited above.

Employment Agencies

Most employment agencies specialize in a particular segment of the job market. By reading the want ads you can identify employment agencies which list jobs in your career field.

The first thing to ascertain about an employment agency is who is paying for the service. If you are paying for the service, the agency will expect a generous percentage of your first year's income if you take a job that it tells you about. If the employer is paying for the service, then there should be no charge to you.

State employment offices will serve you without charge and many now list professional jobs. If you decide to use a state employment service, try to identify a counselor who seems interested in you and make contact with that person every week.

Executive search firms are paid by employers to recruit executives for their company. They are not in business to assist graduates in finding first jobs. Usually they are looking for highly skilled, experienced professionals who might be willing to consider a different position.

Answering Want Ads: Applying for Jobs

In applying for a job, always write a cover letter to send with your resume. Take a day or two to research the position that is listed and to learn about how the search is being conducted. Try to get information about the employer and about the job. If it is a large company, you can obtain a copy of an annual report and other information as you would for an on-campus recruiter, but if it is a small employer, your search may have to rely on interviews with people who know the organization. If your career exploration has been focusing on that type of work, you probably already know somebody who can give you information about the employer.

Many want ads request that the applicant have three to five years of experience. If you do not have any full-time work experience in the field, you can still apply, but you must describe how your paid and unpaid experiences have prepared you for this job.

Listed jobs represent only a small portion of the job market. You should check the job listings in your field at regular intervals, but your greatest investment of time and energy should be in initiating contact with potential employers.

IDENTIFYING AND CONTACTING POTENTIAL EMPLOYERS

Taking the initiative to contact employers for whom you would like to work is the most important part of your job hunt. Your stated objective in making the contact is to request the opportunity to talk with the potential employer about career opportunities in his field, and to seek his advice on job-hunting strategies. Your parallel agenda is to make personal contact with people who have the power to hire you and to use the opportunity to present your interest in and qualifications for working in their organization. If the interview goes well and the employer is impressed with your potential, he may recommend that you contact some of his colleagues in the same or other organizations.

If each employer that you interview will recommend you to three other potential employers, you will soon develop a network of people in your career field who know of your availability on the job market and are impressed with your qualifications. Especially if your background makes you an unusual candidate, you want to have the opportunity to meet and interview with top executives. It is generally high-level executives who have the overview, the insight, and the power to think creatively about how an unusual candidate might be useful in their organization.

If you have a Ph.D. and are job hunting on the nonacademic job market, it is important that you initiate contact with high-level executives and discuss with them the special contribution you can make to their organization. Read Chapter 3 in *Corporate PhD*, "Landing in the Corporate Corridor," for some inspiration.

How to Identify Potential Employers

From your study of job listings in your career field, you may have several kinds of helpful information. If you have learned about types of jobs that interest you and for which you have applied, you may next try to identify other employers who might have similar types of jobs. If an employer is advertising jobs that are too advanced for you, you might contact that employer anyway, because he might promote someone from within and then have a lower-level job opening for which you would be qualified. If your chosen type of employer is not listing jobs in any resource that you have studied, do not despair; for a variety of reasons some employers do not list jobs publicly.

People are the best source of names of potential employers. Return to the career advisers whom you contacted during your exploration period to request advice about job-hunting strategies and ask if they can refer you to colleagues in their career field.

To generate personal contacts in your chosen career field, you should talk to everyone about your job objectives: your academic adviser, your tutor, your former employers, your friends, your friends' parents, your family, your neighbors. A personal referral increases the likelihood that you will get an interview with a potential employer. Once in the interview, however, you are on your own. You will be hired only if you convince the employer that you are the best person for the job.

Every career field has directories which list organizations and give information about them. From a directory you can learn the names of executives of the organization, addresses, and other information. For large companies, you should write to the manager of the division in which you would like to work. For a middle-size company, you should write to the chief executive officer.

In the professional journals of your chosen field, you can learn about potential employers: persons who are mentioned in news articles; persons who are interviewed by the journal; and persons who write articles which are published in the journals. When contacting somebody about whom you have read, you should always tell him where you learned his name.

How to Contact Potential Employers

The sections in Chapter 4 on writing resumes and letters give you general advice and samples to assist you in the development of your own resume and letters. It is important that your materials and your style of making contact be appropriate to the industry. The best guideline to how aggressive, assertive, and persistent you should be is your judgment of how much those qualities are valued in the job and the field to which you are applying.

The usual way of making contact with a potential employer is by writing a letter expressing your interest in his organization and career field. You may enclose a resume or introduce yourself in the letter that you write. In some career fields, contact by telephone is acceptable and may be more productive. When an adviser or friend or personal contact gives you a referral, you might ask how you should make the contact. Seek advice in job-hunting strategy and style from your career advisers.

The Employer's Perspective

Employers are interested in young people who have chosen their career field. Most midcareer people enjoy being helpful and giving advice to those who are looking for opportunities in their career field.

Employers will usually consent to interviews with people who have been referred to them by friends or colleagues. If the friend is someone whom they respect, they will agree to the interview with the expectation that you are somebody who will be of interest to them.

Employers look for talent. Most employers, even if they do not have any open jobs at the moment, are interested in identifying people who might be productive members of their organization in the future.

SURVIVING THE JOB HUNT

Job hunting takes time and energy. If you are job hunting full-time, you should plan a work schedule as seriously as if you were being paid to conduct this search. Set objectives for the number of employers you will write to and the number of interviews you will schedule each week. Develop a daily routine of interviews in the morning, lunch with friends, library research in the afternoon, and letter writing or other reading in the evening—or whatever makes sense for you. But make a schedule and keep to it.

If you are job hunting while you are still a college student or graduate student, set aside a half-day or more each week to devote to your job hunt.

If you are employed, you can do your research and letter writing in the evenings and on weekends, but you will probably have to arrange to take time off for interviews.

If you are job hunting full-time, be realistic about your financial needs. If you do not have savings to support yourself for several months, you will probably want to take a part-time job, something temporary like clerical work or waiting on tables.

Most job markets are very competitive. With each job you apply for, there will be many candidates and you are more likely to be rejected than to be selected. Although it takes a great deal of energy, it is always best to be pursuing several jobs simultaneously. Even when you are a final candidate for a job, you should continue making applications to new jobs. Maybe you will generate several job offers at once and can choose the one that suits you best.

Job hunting can be discouraging. It is hard to keep up your morale when you are not getting positive responses to your letters or positive outcomes to your interviews. Job hunters need friends to share their ups and downs. Find someone who is willing to listen as you relate your experiences. Talking about your interviews and your observations can help you assess these experiences and revise your plans accordingly. Checking in with your career counselor at regular intervals provides the opportunity for you to review your progress and think together about the next step.

If you have been job hunting full-time for two or three months and have not had a job offer, you may want to broaden either your job objective or your geographic area. You do not need to stop applying for your first-choice type of job, but broadening your objectives may result in an earlier job offer.

Working as a volunteer can give you relevant experience. It can bolster your self-confidence and provide the opportunity to work with people in your chosen field. It may also lead to paid employment.

Undertaking an aggressive job hunt increases the likelihood of your getting the job you want. Do not underestimate, however, the element of chance in job hunting. Getting the job that launches your career by being in the right place at the right time and knowing the right people may be the result of chance. It is more often the end result of a carefully planned career exploration and job hunt.

SOURCES

Directories

General

CPC Annual. College Placement Council, Inc., Bethlehem, PA, annual. 4 volumes.
Volume 1 offers general advice on careers and job hunting; volume 2 profiles employers seeking candidates for business and administrative positions; volume 3 does the same for technical positions; volume 4 provides information on employers seeking graduates in health care fields.

CPC National Directory: Who's Who in Career Planning, Placement, and Recruitment. College Placement Council, Inc., Bethlehem, PA, annual.
Lists recruiting personnel at colleges and corporate and government college relations/human resources recruitment personnel. Geographic index of employers.

The Directory of Executive Recruiters. Kennedy Publications, Fitzwilliam, NH, annual.
Introductory information for candidates and clients, followed by separate sections for retainer firms and contingency firms, each indexed by function and industry. Geographic and key principals indexes.

Minority Organizations: A National Directory, 3rd edition. Garrett Park Press, Garrett Park, MD, 1987.
Alphabetical listing of groups established by or serving Native Americans, Blacks, Hispanics, and Asian Americans. Geographic, racial/ethnic, topical, and functional indexes. Bibliography.

Places Rated Almanac: Your Guide to Finding the Best Places to Live in America. Richard Boyer and David Savageau. Prentice Hall, New York, NY, 1989.
Describes and ranks U.S. metropolitan areas on various factors. A good place to begin if you are contemplating a change of scenery!

Research Centers Directory. Karen Hill, editor. Gale Research Inc., Detroit, MI, annual. 2 volumes.
Subject listing of nonprofit research organizations, giving information on research activities and fields, as well as publications, services, and staff size. Subject and alphabetic indexes. Updated by *New Research Centers*.

Arts and Media

Artist's Market: Where & How to Sell Your Artwork. Susan Conner, editor. Writer's Digest Books, Cincinnati, OH, annual.

Introductory chapter on "The Business of Art," followed by a classified listing of the markets, from advertising to syndicates. Includes interviews with successful artists and art buyers. Bibliography, glossary, art/design studio subject and geographic indexes, magazine subject index, general index.

Back Stage TV/Film & Tape Directory. Back Stage Publications, Inc., New York, NY, annual.

Classified listings of production and post production companies and industry-related services. Includes some Canadian listings, as well as more extensive international listings for film commissions.

Billboard International Buyer's Guide. BPI Publications, Inc., New York, NY, annual.

Record companies, video, music publishers, services, organizations, etc., for the music industry.

The Creative Black Book. Friendly Press, Inc., New York, NY, annual. 3 volumes.

Suppliers, photographers, printers, designers, agencies, and services, etc., involved in print and broadcast advertising in North America.

Editor and Publisher International Yearbook. Editor & Publisher, New York, NY, annual.

Geographic listings of: daily, weekly, and specialized newspapers in the U.S. and Canada; general interest newspapers in the rest of the world. Includes information on services, organizations, education, foreign correspondents in the U.S., etc. Indexed.

Handel's National Directory for the Performing Arts, 4th edition. NDPA, Inc., Dallas, TX, 1988. 2 volumes.

Volume 1 lists organizations and facilities geographically, and is indexed by arts area (dance, instrumental music, vocal music, theatre, performing series, facility). Volume 2 lists educational institutions geographically, with dance, music, and theatre indexes. Each volume also has a general index.

Hollywood Creative Directory. Santa Monica, CA, three times yearly.

Alphabetically lists motion picture and TV development and production companies and staff; cross-references companies with studio deals; name index.

International Directory of Arts. Art Address Verlag Mueller GmbH & Co., Frankfurt am Main, Federal Republic of Germany, biennial. 2 volumes.

Museums, schools, associations, artists, numismatists, art and antique dealers, galleries, auctioneers, restorers, art publishers, periodicals, and antiquarian and art booksellers, each arranged by country.

The International Directory of Little Magazines and Small Presses. Len Fulton, editor. Dustbooks, Paradise, CA, annual.

Alphabetical listing, with regional and subject indexes.

International Motion Picture Almanac. Quigley Publishing Co., Inc., New York, NY, annual.

Arranged by service, activity, or other category, with facts and figures. Includes a section entitled "Who's Who in Motion Pictures and Television."

International Television and Video Almanac. Quigley Publishing Co., Inc., New York, NY, annual.

Arranged by service, activity, or other category, with facts and figures. Includes a "Who's Who" section.

Literary Market Place. R.R. Bowker Co., New York, NY, annual.

Lists publishers, organizations, events, awards, fellowships and grants, services, etc., for the publishing trade in the U.S. and Canada; includes foreign publishers with U.S. offices. U.S. publishers can be accessed by geographic location, type, and subject matter. Directory of organizations and individuals included in the text (with phone numbers and addresses).

Musical America International Directory of the Performing Arts. ABC Consumer Magazines, Inc., New York, NY, annual.

Arranged by category. Lists orchestras, opera companies, festivals, music publishers, service and professional organizations, music magazines, etc.

News Media Yellow Book of Washington and New York: A Directory of Those Who Report, Write, Edit and Produce the News in the Nation's Government and Business Capitals. Monitor Publishing Co., New York, NY, semiannual.

Divided into ten sections: news services, newspapers, networks, stations, programs, periodicals, newsletters, publishers, associations, and foreign media. Assignment (by news beat), syndicated columnist, program (by subject), periodical (by subject), personnel, and media indexes.

O'Dwyer's Directory of Corporate Communications. J.R. O'Dwyer Co., Inc., New York, NY, annual.

Lists public relations/communications departments of 5,400 companies and associations, including federal government departments, bureaus, agencies, and commissions. Industry and geographic indexes to corporations; geographical index to associations. Includes foreign listings (mostly Canadian).

O'Dwyer's Directory of Public Relations Firms. J.R. O'Dwyer Co., Inc., New York, NY, annual.
Alphabetical listing of firms; entries include principal executives and clients. Specialty, geographic, and client indexes. Includes firms and branches located outside the U.S.

Photographer's Market: Where & How to Sell Your Photographs. Sam A. Marshall, editor. Writer's Digest Books, Cincinnati, OH, annual.
Introductory chapter on "The Business of Photography," followed by a classified listing of the markets, from advertising to stock photo agencies. Includes interviews with professionals in the field. Lists contests and workshops. Glossary. Indexed.

Regional Theatre Directory. Jill Charles, compiler and editor. American Theatre Works, Inc., Dorset, VT, annual.
Geographically arranged listings of theater companies and dinner theaters, with employment and internship information for performers, designers, technicians, and managers. Lists service organizations and resources, with a brief appendix on the employment process. Alphabetical index of theaters and index of "specialty" companies.

Songwriter's Market: Where & How to Market Your Songs. Mark Garvey, editor. Writer's Digest Books, Cincinnati, OH, annual.
Introductory chapter on "The Business of Songwriting," followed by a classified listing of the markets, from advertising to record producers. Includes interviews with music-business professionals who offer insights and advice. Lists organizations, workshops, contests and awards, and publications. Glossary. Indexed.

Spot Radio. Standard Rate and Data Service, Inc., Wilmette, IL, monthly.
Geographical listing of radio stations, with programming information. Call letter index.

Standard Directory of Advertisers: The Advertiser Red Book. National Register Publishing Co., Wilmette, IL, 2 editions annually: classified and geographic.
Lists companies engaged in national or regional advertising, with product and executive information. Describes advertising agencies and media used, amounts spent, etc. Classified edition has alphabetical and separately published geographic indexes. Updated by *Ad Change.*

Standard Directory of Advertising Agencies: The Agency Red Book. National Register Publishing Co., Wilmette, IL, three times yearly.
Alphabetical listing of approximately 6,500 agencies, giving size, dollar amount of billings, names of executives, and in many cases identifying accounts. Special market, geographic, and name indexes. Includes foreign agencies and separate listings for house agencies, media service organizations, sales promotion agencies, and public relations firms. Updated by *Agency News.*

Television & Cable Factbook. Television Digest, Inc., Washington, DC, annual. 2 volumes.

Worldwide listing of television stations, North American cable systems, including U.S. territories, and related products and services. Indexed.

Theatre Profiles: The Illustrated Guide to America's Nonprofit Professional Theatres. Laura Ross, editor. Theatre Communications Group, New York, NY, biennial.

Alphabetical listing of nonprofit resident theater companies, with staff, fiscal, and production information. Name and title indexes.

Writer's Market: Where & How to Sell What You Write. Glenda Tennant Neff, editor. Writer's Digest Books, Cincinnati, OH, annual.

Introductory chapter on the writing profession, followed by a classified listing of the markets, from book publishers to syndicates. Includes interviews with writers and editors. Lists agents and contests and awards. Glossary, book publishers and author's agents subject indexes, general index.

Business

Consultants and Consulting Organizations Directory: A Reference Guide to Concerns and Individuals Engaged in Consultation for Business, Industry and Government. Janice McLean, editor. Gale Research Inc., Detroit, MI, annual. 2 volumes.

Volume 1 lists firms by field of consulting activity. Geographic, consulting activities, personal name, and consulting firms indexes are contained in volume 2. Updated by *New Consultants.*

The Corporate Finance Sourcebook. National Register Publishing Co., Wilmette, IL, annual.

Classified listing of capital funding and management sources, including venture capital firms, banks, pension managers, and accounting firms. Index of firms.

Encyclopedia of Business Information Sources: A Bibliographic Guide to More Than 21,000 Citations Covering Over 1,000 Subjects of Interest to Business Personnel. James Woy, editor. Gale Research Inc., Detroit, MI, biennial.

Includes print, online, organizational, etc., sources of information. An excellent resource for researching a particular business topic or industry.

Harvard Business School Career Guide: Investment Banking. Harvard Business School Career Resources Center, distributed by the Harvard Business School Press, Boston, MA, biennial.

Intended primarily for MBA students, this publication introduces the investment banking field and profiles firms that offer investment banking opportunities. Glossary. Brief annotated bibliography.

Harvard Business School Career Guide: Management Consulting. Harvard Business School Career Resources Center and the Harvard Business School Management Consulting Club, distributed by the Harvard Business School Press, Boston, MA, biennial.

Intended primarily for MBA students, this publication introduces the consulting field, and includes self-descriptions by a number of top firms. Good brief annotated bibliography.

Harvard Business School Career Guide: Marketing. Harvard Business School Career Resources Center and the Harvard Business School Marketing Club, distributed by the Harvard Business School Press, Boston, MA, biennial.

Intended primarily for MBA students, this publication introduces the marketing field and includes profiles of marketing careers with companies noted for their marketing strengths. Brief annotated bibliography.

How to Get the Hot Jobs in Business and Finance. Mary E. Calhoun. Harper & Row, New York, NY, 1988.

Introductory section on job hunting, resumes, interviews, etc., followed by descriptions of the various financial career fields. The appendix lists 500 financial firms. The text is sprinkled with references to suggested readings.

The Insurance Almanac: Who What When and Where in Insurance. Donald E. Wolff, editor. The Underwriter Printing and Publishing Co., Englewood, NJ, annual.

Lists brokers, adjusters, companies, officials, and related organizations, with names of principals. Indexed.

National Directory of Corporate Public Affairs. Arthur C. Close, editor. Columbia Books, Inc., Washington, DC, annual.

Alphabetical listing of companies with public affairs programs; gives people, addresses, and publications. Separate listing of individuals engaged in public affairs programs. Industry and geographic indexes.

The National Directory of Corporate Training Programs. Ray Bard and Susan K. Elliott. Doubleday, New York, NY, 1988.

Alphabetically arranged by company, with information on recruitment, placement, training, etc. Training program, industry, and geographic indexes. Bibliography.

Peterson's Job Opportunities for Business and Liberal Arts Graduates. Peterson's Guides, Princeton, NJ, annual.

Profiles companies that plan to hire business, social science, and humanities graduates; has an introductory section on the job search and an excellent resource section. Includes starting location, internship, summer, training program, and other special interest indexes.

Pratt's Guide to Venture Capital Sources. Jane K. Morris, Susan Isenstein, and Ann Knowles, editors. Venture Economics, Inc., Needham, MA, annual.

Excellent introductory section on the venture capital industry, followed by geographically arranged listings of venture capital companies in the U.S. and Canada. Company, name, and industry preference indexes.

The Rand McNally Banker's Directory. Rand McNally & Co., Skokie, IL, semiannual. 3 volumes.

Volumes 1 and 2 list banks geographically within the U.S. and include names of officers and financial data. Alphabetical index. Volume 3 contains geographic listings of international banks in foreign exchange/trade (other than those in U.S. locations), and has an alphabetical index.

Reference Book of Corporate Managements. Dun's Marketing Services, Inc., Parsippany, NJ, annual. 4 volumes.

Biographical profiles of the principal officers in over 12,000 U.S. companies. Arranged alphabetically by company, with geographic, industry, and personal name indexes.

Sports Market Place. Richard A. Lipsey, editor. Sportsguide, Inc., Princeton, NJ, annual, with supplement.

Lists associations, teams, publications, broadcasters, promoters, suppliers, etc. Product, brand name, executive, geographic, and master indexes. A good source for anyone interested in identifying sports-related career possibilities.

Standard & Poor's Register of Corporations, Directors and Executives. Standard & Poor's Corp., New York, NY, annual, with triennial supplement. 3 volumes.

Volume 1 lists U.S. corporations alphabetically, naming principal executives; volume 2 lists directors and executives alphabetically, giving very brief biographical information where available; volume 3 contains industrial, geographic, and corporate family indexes.

Standard & Poor's Security Dealers of North America. Standard & Poor's Corp., New York, NY, semiannual.

Geographically arranged, with index of firms. Geographic listing of foreign offices.

Training and Development Organizations Directory, 4th edition. Janice McLean, editor. Gale Research Inc., Detroit, MI, 1988.

Alphabetically profiles firms, institutes, etc. Geographic, personal name, and subject indexes.

U.S. Real Estate Register. Barry, Inc., Wilmington, MA, annual.

Alphabetical listing of real estate and industrial development companies; classified listing of related services and organizations. Selected international listings for some categories.

Education

Directory of Public School Systems in the U.S. Association for School, College and University Staffing, Inc., Addison, IL, annual.
Lists school districts and employing officials by state.

The Handbook of Private Schools: An Annual Descriptive Survey of Independent Education. Porter Sargent Publishers, Inc., Boston, MA, annual.
Geographically arranged listing of leading private schools, with separate listings for schools abroad, summer camps and programs, etc. Index of schools.

Private Independent Schools. Bunting and Lyon, Inc., Wallingford, CT, annual.
Geographically arranged listing includes American programs in other countries and U.S. territories; separate section for summer programs, including sports, the arts, etc. Index of schools.

Government, Health, Human Services, and Law

The Almanac of American Politics. Michael Barone and Grant Ujifusa. National Journal, Washington, DC, annual.
Contains basic information on elections, individuals, and events, from the Presidency and Congress through the state level. Detailed data on congressional districts and their representatives, and separate chapters on demographics and campaign finance. Indexed.

Congressional Staff Directory. Ann L. Brownson, editor. Congressional Staff Directory, Ltd., Mount Vernon, VA, semiannual.
Information on key personnel of the legislative branch. Congressional staff biographies; keyword index; index of individuals.

Congressional Yellow Book. Monitor Publishing Co., Washington, DC, quarterly.
Profiles members of Congress and congressional committees; includes information on aides and congressional support agencies (such as the Library of Congress).

Directory of Opportunities in International Law, 8th edition. Willard A. Stanback, editor-in-chief. John Bassett Moore Society of International Law, Charlottesville, VA, 1987.
Geographical listing of firms, followed by alphabetical listings of agencies, organizations, and academic programs. Bibliography.

Encyclopedia of Medical Organizations and Agencies, 2nd edition. Anthony T. Kruzas, Kay Gill, and Robert Wilson, editors. Gale Research Co., Detroit, MI, 1987.
"A Subject Guide to More than 11,000 Medical Societies, Professional and Voluntary Associations, Foundations, Research Institutes, Federal and State Agencies, Medical and Allied Health Schools, Information Centers, Data Base Services, and Related Health Care Organizations." Master name and keyword index.

Federal Executive Directory. Carroll Publishing Co., Washington, DC, bimonthly.
Telephone numbers, names, addresses, and titles for individuals in the executive branch and Congress. Keyword index.

Federal Regional Executive Directory. Carroll Publishing Co., Washington, DC, semiannual.
Information on federal regional offices, home state offices of members of Congress, key personnel of federal courts, and contacts for military bases. Name, keyword, and geographic indexes.

Federal Regulatory Directory, 5th edition. Congressional Quarterly, Inc., Washington, DC, 1986.
Profiles regulatory agencies within the federal government, including names of contacts. Name and subject indexes.

Federal Yellow Book. Monitor Publishing Co., Washington, DC, quarterly.
Arranged by department or agency, lists names and telephone numbers of top people in the executive branch of the federal government. Indexed.

Great Careers: The Fourth of July Guide to Careers, Internships, and Volunteer Opportunities in the Nonprofit Sector. Devon Cottrell Smith, editor. Garrett Park Press, Garrett Park, MD, 1990.
Lists resources and organizations by topic/career area from animal rights to women's issues. Includes essays on various issues associated with work in the not-for-profit sector. Chapter indexes and general index of resources and organizations.

Law and Legal Information Directory. Steven Wasserman, Jacqueline Wasserman O'Brien, and Bonnie Shaw Pfaff, editors. Gale Research Inc., Detroit, MI, biennial. 2 volumes.
Organizations, courts, agencies, schools, funding sources, libraries, research centers, publications, etc., arranged by category. Some sections have indexes.

Municipal Executive Directory. Wil Woodrum, editor. Carroll Publishing Co., Washington, DC, semiannual.
Alphabetically lists key executives of over 2,000 municipalities with populations over 1,000. Alphabetical listing of executives; includes listings for related national associations, state municipal associations, and members of the National Association of Towns and Townships. Geographic index.

National Directory of Children and Youth Services. Marion L. Peterson. Longmont, CO, biennial.

Part 1 is a state-by-state listing of public and private services and agencies; part 2 lists federal and national organizations and clearinghouses; part 3 is a buyer's guide to specialized services and products.

National Directory of Private Social Agencies. Helga B. Croner, Croner Publications, Inc., Queens Village, NY, 1990, with monthly supplements.

Geographically arranged, with index of services. Very little information beyond address and telephone numbers, but it identifies some fairly obscure services.

National Health Directory. Aspen Systems Corp., Rockville, MD, annual.

Identifies policymakers in federal and state agencies, as well as city and county health officials. Name indexes.

Politics in America. Alan Ehrenhalt, editor. Congressional Quarterly, Inc., Washington, DC, biennial.

Profiles of senators and representatives, including committee assignments and votes on key issues, with introductory information on each state and its government. Indexed.

The Public Interest Handbook: A Guide to Legal Careers In Public Interest Organizations. Geoffrey Kaiser and Barbara Mulé. Locust Hill Press, West Cornwall, CT, 1987.

Geographically arranged profiles of organizations provide employment information, including summer and volunteer opportunities. Appendixes list public interest legal organizations, public defender offices, public interest law firms, and labor organizations. Alphabetical and area of specialization indexes.

Public Interest Profiles, 1988-1989. Foundation for Public Affairs. Congressional Quarterly, Inc., Washington, DC, 1988.

Profiles public interest and public policy organizations. Arranged by field of interest; includes think tanks. Good coverage of each group provides budget information, staff size, operating method, publication lists, etc. Group and name indexes.

State Executive Directory. Carroll Publishing Co., Washington, DC, three times yearly.

State-by-state listing of state government officials, including telephone numbers. Separate section for legislative committees and officers. Personal name and keyword indexes.

State Municipal League Directory. National League of Cities. Washington, DC, annual.

Describes the municipal leagues in existence for the continental states. Includes league publications which sometimes carry job opportunities for member municipalities.

State Yellow Book: A Directory of the Executive, Legislative and Judicial Branches of the 50 State Governments. Monitor Publishing Co., New York, NY, semiannual.
Includes state profiles and intergovernmental organizations. Subject and name (by state) indexes.

The United States Government Manual. Office of the Federal Register, National Archives and Records Administration, Washington, DC, annual.
Official handbook of the U.S. government; describes departments and agencies, lists key personnel, and provides organization charts. Name and subject/agency indexes. Includes information on quasi-official agencies, international organizations in which the U.S. participates, boards, committees, and commissions. The place to start for information on the federal government.

Washington 90: A Comprehensive Directory of the Key Institutions and Leaders of the National Capital Area. Columbia Books, Inc., Washington, DC, annual.
Classified arrangement of institutions, law firms, the media, governmental units, and other organizations in Washington. Index of organizations and individuals. (Title changes with year.)

Washington Information Directory. Congressional Quarterly Inc., Washington, DC, annual.
Classified arrangement of information services in the public and nonprofit sectors in the Washington area, including names of officials and brief statement of mission. Name and subject indexes.

Washington Representatives: Who Does What for Whom in the Nation's Capital. Columbia Books, Inc., Washington, DC, annual.
Alphabetical listing of individuals who work for American trade associations, professional societies, labor unions, corporations, and public interest groups, followed by an alphabetical listing of companies and organizations. Subject and foreign interest indexes.

Science and Technology

Conservation Directory: A List of Organizations, Agencies, and Officials Concerned with Natural Resource Use and Management. National Wildlife Federation, Washington, DC, annual.
Includes international, national, and interstate commissions and organizations, as well as U.S. and Canadian government and citizens' groups. Lists colleges and universities, conservation/environment offices of foreign governments, additional resources, etc. Subject and name indexes.

Directory of American Research and Technology: Organizations Active in Product Development for Business. R.R. Bowker, New York, NY, annual.

Alphabetical listing of nongovernment facilities involved in research and development, including subsidiaries. Information on staff and research fields. Geographic, personnel, and classified indexes.

The Directory of Massachusetts High Technology Companies. Mass Tech Times, Inc. Watertown, MA, annual.

Lists manufacturing, research, engineering, consulting, and software firms. Names key personnel. Product, software applications, staff size, and geographic indexes.

New England Directory for Computer Professionals. The Bradford Co., Scituate, MA, annual.

Alphabetical listing of companies with MIS/DP departments. Identifies DP managers and systems/computers on site. Geographic index.

Peterson's Job Opportunities for Engineering, Science, and Computer Graduates. Peterson's Guides, Princeton, NJ, annual.

Contains profiles of selected employers, and has an excellent resource section. Includes starting location, internship, summer, training program, and other special interest indexes.

State-by-State Biotechnology Directory: Centers, Companies, and Contacts. Biotechnology Information Division of the North Carolina Biotechnology Center. The Bureau of National Affairs, Inc., Washington, DC, 1990.

Geographically lists state government contacts, nonprofit research centers, and companies actually working with new technologies. Lists some federal contacts. Company index.

World Environmental Directory, North America, 5th edition. Business Publishers, Inc., Silver Spring, MD, 1989.

Lists companies, agencies, and organizations, including attorneys with environmental interests, corporate environmental officials, educational institutions, and grants. Separate sections for international and Canadian organizations. Personnel index.

Handbooks

The Back Stage Handbook for Performing Artists. Sherry Eaker, compiler and editor. Back Stage Books, New York, NY, 1989.

Discusses resumes, portfolios, the job hunt, and employment possibilities for actors, singers, and dancers. Lists training opportunities. Indexed.

Becoming a Designer: Leading Design Professionals Talk Candidly about What It Takes to Get Started and Succeed as a Graphic Designer. Karen Buffenbarger, editor. Impact Studio, Arcata, CA, 1989.

Profiles 40 California design studios, including design departments of advertising agencies and publishing firms. Provides in chart form basic information about the firms, including hiring policies, computer equipment, and internship opportunities. Lists resources.

A Career Guide for PhD's and PhD Candidates in English and Foreign Languages. Revised by English Showalter. Modern Language Association of America, New York, NY, 1985.

Describes both academic and nonacademic job searches, with sample letters, curricula vitae, and resumes. Lists some additional resources.

Career Planning Guide for International Students. Jane Etish-Andrews, Kerry Anne Santry, and Steve Sjoberg, editors. International Careers Consortium, Boston, MA, 1989.

Discusses career planning, the job search process (in both the U.S. and abroad), immigration and legal issues, work in the U.S., and return to the home culture. Lists resources.

Careers in Secret Operations: How to Be a Federal Intelligence Officer. David Atlee Phillips. Stone Trail Press, Bethesda, MD, 1984.

Describes the employment process and profiles intelligence organizations. Chapters on ethics, retirement, and terminology. Annotated bibliography.

Design Career: Practical Knowledge for Beginning Illustrators and Graphic Designers. Van Nostrand Reinhold Co., New York, NY, 1987.

Includes case histories and an extensive annotated resource list. Indexed.

Finding a Job in Your Field: A Handbook for Ph.D.'s and M.A.'s. Rebecca Anthony and Gerald Roe. Peterson's Guides, Princeton, NJ, 1984.

Aimed primarily at the academic job market, although it does discuss other types of employment. Covers practical matters, such as letters, resumes, vitae, interviewing, evaluating offers, etc. Appendixes on accrediting associations and academic and professional associations.

How to Get a Job in Advertising. Ken Haas. Art Direction Book Co., New York, NY, 1979.

A job-hunting handbook which focuses on the different career possibilities and search strategies within the broad field of advertising. Includes a glossary of advertising terms.

How to Land a Job in Journalism. Phil Swann and Ed Achorn. Betterway Publications, Inc., White Hall, VA, 1988.
>Includes chapters on resumes and cover letters and interviewing, as well as case histories. Indexed.

How to Put Your Book Together and Get a Job in Advertising. Maxine Paetro. The Copy Workshop, Chicago, IL, 1990.
>A guide to compiling a portfolio, with job-hunting hints specific to advertising; includes interviews with creative people in the field.

Inside Management Training: The Career Guide to Training Programs for College Graduates. Marian L. Salzman with Deidre A. Sullivan. New American Library, New York, NY, 1985.
>Introductory information on job hunting, followed by descriptions of training programs grouped by industry, including public service employers. Appendix lists leading employers in various industries geographically. Excellent annotated bibliography.

Inside Track: How to Get into and Succeed in America's Prestige Companies. Ross Petras and Kathryn Petras. Vintage Books, New York, NY, 1986.
>Introduces various career fields, and profiles two to five major employers within each field. Includes comments from individuals working in various positions for the employers profiled.

Job Hunting for the Disabled. Edith Marks and Adele Lewis. Barron's Educational Series, Inc., Woodbury, NY, 1983.
>Discusses identification of skills and the job hunt, focusing on legal and practical issues. Appendixes list publications and organizations of interest to individuals with disabilities.

Money Jobs! Training Programs Run by Banking, Accounting, Insurance, and Brokerage Firms—and How to Get into Them. Marti Prashker and S. Peter Valiunas. Crown Publishers, Inc., New York, NY, 1984.
>Overview of the financial services industry, with a chapter on each of the five kinds of financial institutions: commercial banks, investment banks, accounting firms, diversified financial institutions, and insurance companies. Profiles major employers in each field and describes their entry-level jobs and training programs. Bibliography and glossary. Indexed.

Take Charge: A Strategic Guide for Blind Job Seekers. Rami Rabby and Diane Croft. National Braille Press Inc., Boston, MA, 1989.
>Available in print, Braille, casette, IBM disk, and VersaBraille II editions, this book offers valuable advice on self-assessment, career exploration, the job hunt, and surviving on the job. Much of the information is appropriate for *any* job seeker, not just those with visual and/or other disabilities. Lists resources.

Indexes

Business Periodicals Index. H.W. Wilson Co., Bronx, NY, monthly, with annual cumulations.

Indexes English-language business periodicals, with a separate listing of citations to book reviews. A good way to look up current information on potential employers, assuming you have access to the periodicals indexed.

Current Index to Journals in Education. Oryx Press, Phoenix, AZ, under contract with the U.S. Office of Education's Educational Resources Information Center (ERIC), monthly, with semiannual cumulations.

Indexes articles in nearly 800 education and education-related journals. Subject, author, and journal content indexes.

Predicasts Forecasts. Predicasts Inc., Cleveland, OH, quarterly, with annual cumulations.

Abstracts articles and special reports on U.S. corporations, industries, and products, including those appearing in selected foreign publications. An excellent way to research potential employers and business-related career fields.

The Readers Guide to Periodical Literature. The H.W. Wilson Co., New York, NY, 17 times a year, cumulated annually.

Author and subject index to general interest periodicals published in the United States, including titles in the arts, business, education, government, health, music, and science.

Skills Development

Essentials of Accounting, 4th edition. Robert N. Anthony. Addison-Wesley Publishing Co., Reading, MA, 1988.

A programmed text requiring about 25 hours to complete, including tests. Covers the basic concepts of accounting.

Harcourt Brace Jovanovich College Outline Series. Harcourt Brace Jovanovich, New York, NY.

Volumes on computers, statistics, etc., offer course material in outline form, along with sample problems and tests.

Schaum's Outline Series. McGraw-Hill Book Co., New York, NY.

Numerous titles in the fields of accounting, business and economics, computers, mathematics, statistics, etc. Each outline gives basic theory, definitions, and sample problems.

Chapter 4

JOB-HUNTING SKILLS

WRITING A RESUME

What Is a Resume?

A resume is career-related history directed to a specific audience for a specific purpose. It is not your life story. The resume is a presentation in outline form of your education, work, and other experiences which describes accomplishments that highlight your qualifications for employment.

The purpose of a resume is to introduce yourself to prospective employers. The objective is to present your qualifications clearly and succinctly so that the employer will want to interview you. The resume is also a record of your name, address, telephone number, and pertinent information, which you can leave with every career-related contact person you meet.

The particular mix of qualifications that an employer prefers will depend on the job to be filled. The more you know about what the employer is looking for, the better you can tailor your presentation.

If you are an undergraduate, graduating senior, or graduate student with little or no relevant work experience, your resume will be a presentation that highlights your general qualifications as well as your specific skills. Your resume should document your ability to

- learn quickly
- adapt to new environments
- research, analyze, and solve problems
- initiate and develop new programs

- work cooperatively and collaboratively
- lead a team
- follow instructions
- make efficient use of time
- deal with ambiguity
- make decisions
- communicate effectively
- meet deadlines
- receive recognition for outstanding achievement.

Employers look for people who are enthusiastic, energetic, reliable, mature, productive, perceptive, intelligent, persistent, conscientious, and ambitious.

Preparing to Write Your Resume

Your resume should be designed for two types of reading: the reviewer who scans your resume should learn your academic degrees, job titles, special experiences, or skills; the reviewer who reads your resume should learn valued information about your achievements and receive an impression of your competencies and your personal qualities.

Developing a good resume is a challenging task. The best resumes are usually a product of many drafts. Start by writing a comprehensive outline of all the experiences and facts you might want to include in your resume. Use this outline as a reference while you experiment with a variety of formats and styles. Select the most pertinent information from the outline. If possible, use a computer or word processor when you are developing your resume, so that you can experiment more easily with different formats.

In order to develop a resume that communicates your qualifications for employment, you need to understand what employers are seeking. Identify several prospective employers and find out what qualifications they value. Reading occupational and company literature gives you a good introduction, but visiting a person at work so you can observe the functions, the pace, the interpersonal relationships, and the work environment will allow you to assess firsthand what qualifications are required.

Ask several kinds of people to read and comment on drafts of your resume. Friends can tell you whether they think you have succeeded in communicating your strengths. Advisers can comment on the impression your resume makes and what they learn about you from it. When you interview career advisers to learn about occupations and gather job-hunting advice, ask them to critique your resume for its appropriateness to their field.

Career counselors can help you identify what employers are looking for and what you have to offer. When you meet with a counselor, bring a draft or drafts of your resume and the comprehensive outline from which you have worked. This will make it easier for the counselor to help you design a presentation which communicates your qualifications effectively.

The following guidelines are distilled from many consultations about resumes with students, job hunters, and employers. Please read carefully and then start experimenting with different formats and styles for your presentation.

Types of Resumes

The format that you choose for your resume should be one which you think best communicates your qualifications. There are three basic types of resumes: chronological, functional/chronological, and functional.

The **chronological resume** presents information in reverse chronological order under each category, i.e., Education, Work Experience, Activities. For example, under Education, you would list your latest academic degree or degree-in-progress first, then other degrees received previously, or study at other universities such as study abroad, and, finally, your secondary school, if relevant. Likewise, under Work Experience, you would list your current or most recent job first and continue in reverse chronological order, listing both your summer and termtime work experience. For consistency, entries under additional sections such as Activities or Travel should also list the most recent activity first.

Some chronological resumes list the dates of each experience in the left margin. This is not required; dates can be listed anywhere. The left margin is prime space that can often be used more effectively to focus attention on job titles or places of employment, as in several of the sample resumes that follow. You can attract the attention of the reader to the jobs or activities that you think are most relevant by writing a longer description of your responsibilities and accomplishments in those positions.

The chronological resume is the most common form of resume, especially for young people. Many employers prefer the chronological resume because it catalogs in straightforward fashion the person's work-related experiences. At a glance, the employer learns your educational background, what you have done each summer, and what activities and work you have engaged in during each academic year.

The **functional/chronological** resume can be very effective in presenting specific career-related skills and achievements that have been gained in a variety of experiences. Functional categories that you might use include public relations, research, teaching, leadership, or management. In each section you would list both paid and unpaid work and activities in which you had developed that type of skill.

The entries within each section should be listed in reverse chronological order. Some positions might be listed in more than one section; for example, the position of Waterfront Director at a camp would describe the teaching aspects of the job under the Teaching section, and the managerial/supervising aspects of the job in a section presenting those skills. Overuse of double entries on this type of resume can seem very redundant. But when carried out successfully, the functional/chronological resume organizes for the employer the information that is most important to him and communicates that the applicant knows what types of qualifications the employer values.

The third type of resume, the **functional resume**, is more frequently used by midcareer people who are interested in changing careers. The first part of the resume lists accomplishments and/or qualifications in short, action-oriented statements which are usually highlighted with a bullet or asterisk. The second part provides a summary of work history with dates, names of employers, and job titles. Sometimes a very impressive list of achievements, documented with size of budget, number of employees, volume of sales, etc., can be extracted from years of work in a variety of jobs and presented in the functional part of the resume.

One difficulty with this type of resume is that, in order to assess the value or relevance of an accomplishment or activity, an employer must know the context in which it occurred. Therefore, it is important that the writer indicate the position with which each accomplishment is connected.

A fourth variation sometimes used by persons who are concerned about their age is to remove all the dates from their resumes. The dateless resume seems to bring out the Sherlock Holmes in many of us; the employer's search for a clue which would indicate the person's age can often distract him from noting the person's qualifications.

Format

Most employers prefer a one-page resume. This preference is particularly notable in business. These employers want an effectively organized and concise presentation of the most pertinent information about you. Employers in education, public service, and human services do not seem to have a strong preference, but a concise presentation shows that you respect the value of their time. Remember that a resume is an example of your work. If you claim skills in organization and the ability to communicate clearly and concisely, your resume should demonstrate your proficiency in those skills. Advice on whether a one-page resume is preferred by the employers you are targeting is available from counselors and career advisers.

Resume preparation requires careful thought and discipline. You must make judgements about what is most important and allot space accordingly. Descriptions of jobs and accomplishments must be brief and listing of activities selective. If you decide you cannot fit your resume on one page, put all of the most important information on the first page. Certain information that is often included in longer resumes, such as a list of publications or a list of references, may be presented separately as attachments if you decide they are important to your application. Other attachments may include an annotated transcript, clippings, writing samples, portfolio, and letters of recommendation.

As you experiment with different formats for your resume, make purposeful use of capitals, boldface, underlining, positioning, and spacing. If you have your resume produced on a laser printer, you have many styles and sizes of type from which to choose. Beware of using too-small type, as you may reduce your readership. White or ecru paper is preferred, and you should purchase matching envelopes and paper for your cover letters. Do not try to dazzle your potential employer by using brightly colored paper. It will overshadow your message and is very likely to land in the circular file.

Style

Style also communicates a message. Staccato phrases and action words such as "Designed data collection system. Analyzed data and prepared sixty-page report," give an efficient, goal-oriented impression. For some individuals, however, the flow of complete sentences is more suitable. Whichever style you choose, *be consistent*. Use the same sentence structure and format in every description.

The appearance of your resume makes a strong impression. It should be neat, uncrowded, attractive, and easy to read. Accuracy in use of language, information, and spelling is very important. If you do not have access to a word processor, hire someone who does. Check and double-check to make sure there are absolutely no errors. You might want to use the method of some proofreaders: read the final version aloud while another person reads the original silently.

Content

It is expected that your resume will contain your name, address, and telephone number, and information about your education and work experience. Other sections, titles, and arrangements are at your discretion.

Education and experience are usually presented in reverse chronological order. Within this structure you should give the most space to the most important experience. For example, the work experience which is most relevant to the job you are seeking or which demonstrates a skill valued in a particular field should have the longest description, as this will attract the reader's attention.

The discussion below is general advice. Remember your resume should be designed to give the best presentation of *your qualifications*.

Name, Address, and Telephone. This is the most important information on the resume. Be sure this information is accurate so that employers can contact you. Usually it is centered and in capital letters at the top of the page. If you must give a temporary (school) address and home address, place your name at the top center and the addresses to the right and left. It is not advisable to put your name in the left-hand corner, as it will be obscured when a pile of resumes are clipped together.

Education. If you are a student or have recently completed an academic degree, it is best to put this section first. List your college or university degree or degree expected and date, your concentration, subject of senior honors thesis if written, and electives which are relevant to your employers. Include selected honors if you have received recognition for outstanding academic work. Ph.D. students should list their department, area of interest, relevant electives, and selected honors. The dissertation topic may be included if of related interest.

Secondary school is usually listed on undergraduate resumes. If you went to public high school, listing your secondary school tells employers where you are from. If you went to private school, listing your school will enable you to tap an alumni network. Space devoted to honors and/or activities should depend on their contribution to the total message.

Work Experience. This section, which is usually the major section, can be called "Work Experience" or "Experience" and should include all experience, paid and unpaid, and extracurricular activities which have given you the opportunity to develop the kinds of skills and qualifications that employers seek. You may mix paid and unpaid, part-time and full-time positions, but you should note in some way what the time commitment was. Your experiences should be listed in reverse chronological order, drawing attention to your most important experience by the length of description. For some people it is effective to list experience by career-related functions in order to highlight relevant experience.

The job title, organization, and address should be listed prominently, followed by a concise description of functions performed and goals achieved. Write descriptions in the vocabulary of the industry to which you are applying. Describe first the function which was most challenging and interesting, not necessarily the one at which you spent most of your time. Use action verbs such as those on the list at the end of this section to state what responsibilities you carried out, and use numbers to communicate the magnitude of your achievements; for example:

- managed a $10,000 budget
- sold 20% more space than any other summer employee each month
- supervised installation of new computer system, adapted software and trained 10 staff users
- recruited, trained, and supervised 25 volunteer tutors
- edited and prepared for publication a 200-page report on toxic waste
- made all arrangements for transportation and living accommodations for the Glee Club's six-week tour in Europe

Avoid the expression "Responsible for —"; this does not communicate that tasks were completed or that anything was achieved. Listing the name of a reference person and telephone number with each job is not necessary. If you have letters of reference from the supervisors of your most responsible positions, you may want to attach them.

Activities. College activities can be listed and described under "Education," "Experience," "Activities," or most briefly under "Personal Background," depending on how much emphasis and space you want to give them. If you have held leadership positions, responsibilities for organizing or initiating new programs, financial management or any kind of career-related experiences, be sure they are clearly described. Explain for the reader what the organization is—for example, *"The Independent,* a weekly news magazine"; "House Committee, student government in my residential unit of 350 students."

Languages. Make a separate category to list language skills if you are fluent and hope to use these skills on the job. Computer languages may also be listed in this section.

Travel. Experience traveling, working, or studying abroad should be described explicitly if job related and should be mentioned on any resume because it documents experience in adjusting to different cultures. If you decide not to have a "Travel" section, you can mention travel under "Personal Background."

Skills. If you have specific job-related skills such as computer programming or foreign language fluency, you may want to list them in a "Skills" section.

Interests. Save at least one line for a list of avocational interests such as "reading science fiction, playing guitar, choral singing, and running." Even a brief list rounds out your presentation and may establish an initial bond of common interest with the reader.

Personal Background. On a one-page resume you have had to leave out a great deal. This section may be used to mention information that you consider important: "To help pay college expenses have worked every term delivering newspapers, washing dishes, bartending, driving a shuttle bus." "Lived in a small town in Ohio until I came to Harvard." "Born and grew up in New York City." (Where you spent your youth may be an important message to the employer.) "Played varsity lacrosse and intramural basket-ball."

Job Objective. Only if you have a clearly defined employment goal should you write a job objective. The cover letter is the preferred place to state your job objective, so that you can tailor it to each job application and highlight and expand on relevant information from the resume.

Action Words. This list may help you describe your accomplishments in your paid and unpaid work experiences.

Accelerated	Conducted	Generated
Accomplished	Constructed	Guided
Achieved	Controlled	Halved
Acted	Coordinated	Headed
Added	Counseled	Hired
Administered	Created	Identified
Advised	Defined	Implemented
Analyzed	Delivered	Improved
Appointed	Demonstrated	Improvised
Arranged	Designed	Increased
Assembled	Determined	Initiated
Assessed	Developed	Inspected
Audited	Doubled	Instituted
Averted	Earned	Instructed
Bought	Edited	Interviewed
Broadened	Eliminated	Introduced
Built	Employed	Invented
Centralized	Established	Launched
Changed	Evaluated	Lectured
Clarified	Examined	Led
Classified	Executed	Located
Collaborated	Expanded	Maintained
Competed	Expedited	Managed
Compiled	Fabricated	Marketed
Composed	Followed	Minimized
Computed	Formed	Monitored
Conceived	Formulated	Motivated
Concluded	Founded	Negotiated

Operated	Represented	Surpassed
Organized	Researched	Surveyed
Originated	Resolved	Synthesized
Participated	Reversed	Taught
Performed	Reviewed	Terminated
Persuaded	Revised	Tested
Planned	Scheduled	Tightened
Predicted	Selected	Traced
Prepared	Served	Trained
Prevented	Settled	Translated
Processed	Shaped	Trimmed
Programmed	Simplified	Tripled
Promoted	Sold	Uncovered
Proposed	Solved	Unified
Proved	Staffed	Unraveled
Provided	Started	Utilized
Published	Stimulated	Verbalized
Purchased	Strengthened	Verified
Recommended	Stretched	Visualized
Recruited	Structured	Widened
Redesigned	Studied	Withdrew
Reduced	Summarized	Won
Renegotiated	Supervised	Worked
Reorganized	Supported	Wrote
Reported		

Sample Resumes

The following sample resumes are fictionalized. They have been selected to represent a variety of formats and styles. We hope they will help you decide how you want to organize information, create emphasis, and describe your accomplishments. However, you should remember that your resume is a personal document. Develop a format and a style that best communicates your attributes for the job you seek.

JEANNE ANDERSON

School Address
Lowell N-12
Harvard University
Cambridge, MA 02138
(617) 555-8778

Permanent Address
24 Ridge Avenue
University City, MO 63130
(314) 555-9990

Education:

> **Harvard University.** Freshman studying psychology and history. Dean's list last semester.
>
> **University City High School.** Salutatorian. National Honor Society. National Merit Finalist. University City Chamber of Commerce Student of the Year.

Experience:

> **TENNIS INSTRUCTION**
>> Teach tennis to 7th and 8th graders as part of Youth Recreation Volunteer Program. 1990-91.
>
> **CHILD CARE**
>> Work as an assistant in Radcliffe Day Care Center ten hours per week. Took care of neighbor's children two afternoons per week after school and occasionally on weekends.
>
> **COMMUNITY SERVICE**
>> Tutored fourth graders in math one afternoon per week during junior and senior years of high school. Organized school-wide recycling program sophomore year of high school and served as liaison with student organizers in other local area high schools.

Related Information:

> As the oldest child in a large family, accustomed to being in charge of younger children.
>
> Enjoy working with children and willing to work hard.
>
> Attended overnight camp two summers. Energetic participant in all sports activities. Won the "Model Camper" award at Camp Silverlake, Rockaway, NC. 1985.

References: Available on request.

Comments: Jeanne is a freshman applying for camp counselor positions. Rather than use a reverse chronological format that emphasizes employers and job titles, she focuses the attention of the reader on three job-related areas and describes the experiences she has had in each area. She has created a separate section where she provides personal information that would be important considerations for a camp director who is evaluating her qualifications. She has also made a point of stating that she can provide references.

MICHELLE C. ROBBINS

Cabot House J-4
Harvard University
Cambridge, MA 02138
(617) 555-4253

12 North Street
Andover, MA 01810
(508) 555-2456

EDUCATION

HARVARD UNIVERSITY   Cambridge, MA
A.B. in Government expected June 1992. Honors candidate.

MANCHESTER HIGH SCHOOL   Manchester, MA
1988 Graduate. Manchester Scholar. Sole recipient of English, History, Debate, and French Awards.
Winner of several national debate tournaments and President of debate team. Captain, Varsity Field Hockey.
Peer Leader.

EXPERIENCE

NATIONAL DEBATE WORKSHOPS   University of Iowa - Iowa City, IA
Debate Instructor.   Samford University - Birmingham, AL
Taught comprehensive debate technique to 250 high school students at 5 camps. Focused on philosophy,
analytical procedure, and communication skills. Presented daily two-hour lectures and led research
investigations. Instructed individuals in critical thinking, logical development of arguments, persuasive and
clear articulation of position, and projection or positive self-image. Summers 1990, 1989, 1988.

OFFICE OF SENATOR TIMOTHY E. WIRTH (D-CO)   Washington, DC
Press Intern. Assisted press secretary with daily responsibilities. Wrote press releases. Organized
conference calls between Senator and Colorado newspapers and radio stations. Observed press conferences
and briefings. Summer 1990.

WHRB-FM RADIO   Cambridge, MA
Writer/Reporter. Produced daily half-hour news show at WHRB (Harvard Radio -- a student-run, self-
supporting, commercial station broadcasting to metropolitan Boston). Identified and developed pertinent
stories. Wrote and reported special features. Anchored the 6:00 p.m. news. February 1990 - present.

HARVARD STUDENT AGENCIES, INC.   Cambridge, MA
Administrative Assistant. Typed, answered phones, and performed general office duties in student-run
agency serving Harvard community. September 1988 - May 1989.

ACTIVITIES

Member of Government Undergraduate Advisory Council (student-faculty advisory group). Chosen to
represent my residential unit of over 400 people on board of 13 students and 5 faculty. A collaborative effort
to address student concerns, clarify goals, and strengthen government department. 1989-1990.

Volunteer for HAND (Harvard House and Neighborhood Development Program) as assistant to special
needs teacher in classroom, Fall 1989.

Waitress/caterer, termtime and summers 1990, 1989, 1988.

PERSONAL

Interests include reading, biking, skiing, and travel. Particular interest in France developed through study of
the language and extended stays with French families.

Comments: Michelle is a junior applying for summer jobs in government. She
emphasizes her most important experiences by putting the name of her employer
and her job title in boldface type. She describes specific accomplishments in each
of her positions and explains for the non-Harvard reader "inside" terms like WHRB
and HSA. Placing the dates of each position at the end of the description saves space.
Note that "Waitress/caterer" is placed in the "Activities" section because she doesn't
want to give it much space, but does want to let the reader know how she supported
herself.

Dunster House D-11
Harvard University
Cambridge, MA 02138
(617) 555-1775

17 NE 140th
Seattle, WA 98155
(206) 555-1234

EDUCATION

Harvard University, Cambridge, MA
A.B. with honors in Social Studies expected June 1992. Harvard College Scholarship for academic achievement of high distinction. Dean's list all semesters. Coursework: economics, statistics, physics, European history, and political and economic development. Familiarity with Apple MacIntosh, Commodore 64, Microsoft software, and Wordstar.

Lakeside School, Seattle, WA
National Merit Scholar, 1988. Four years of French.

WORK EXPERIENCE

Administrative Assistant

Harvard Student Agencies, Harvard University, Cambridge, MA
Supervised staff in text-processing department. Marketed typesetting service to local business community. Operated laser printing service. Fall 1990-present.

Investigator

Seattle-King County Public Defender Association, Seattle, WA
Interviewed and evaluated witnesses, police officers, and victims. Framed defense strategy with attorneys. Investigated and photographed crime scenes, obtained medical records, subpoenaed witnesses, and delivered in-court testimony. Summer 1990.

Salesman

Outdoor Empire Publishing, Seattle, WA
Conducted phone sales and renewals for nation's largest outdoor weekly. Averaged $20 per hour in commissions. Summers 1989, 1988, 1987.

ACTIVITIES

Intercollegiate Athletics

Harvard Football Team, 1988-89.
Harvard Rugby Club, 1990.

Tutor

Middlesex County Correction Center, Boston, MA
Tutored prison inmates in English and math. Winter 1989.

Assistant Coach

Lakeside Football Team, Seattle, WA
Assisted instruction of offensive and defensive lines. Fall 1989.

Varsity

Lakeside School, Seattle, WA
Wrestling, 1986-88: team captain and league champion, 1988.
Football, 1986-87: Most Inspirational Player Award, 1987.
Tennis, 1986-87: league mixed doubles champion, 1987.
Soccer, 1988.

Travel

Europe and Southern Africa.

Comments: David is a junior applying for summer jobs in business. By listing descriptive titles of his jobs and his activities in the left margin, he highlights the diversity of his experiences. The fact that he participates in both intercollegiate athletics and public service at college is likely to be as important to the potential employer as his work experience.

MARTA T. VUELTA

College Address:
22 Linnaean St., North House
Harvard University
Cambridge, MA 02138
(617) 555-1234

Permanent Address:
Smith Place #44
Jackson Park
Guaynabo, PR 00657
(809) 555-0102

EDUCATION

HARVARD UNIVERSITY, Cambridge, MA
B.A. in Psychology with Honors and Teacher Certification to teach high school expected
June 1991.
COMMONWEALTH HIGH SCHOOL, Hato Rey, PR
Named Salutatorian and received Principal's Award for Leadership.

EXPERIENCE

UNITED WAY OF MASS BAY, Boston, MA
Coordinator of the Student Volunteer Resource Center. Assisted schools with the
development of student volunteer programs. Published the College Volunteer Contacts
Listing. Conducted interviews of potential student volunteers. May 1989 to Jan. 1990.

HARVARD UNIVERSITY, Psychology Department, Cambridge, MA
Research Assistant to Professor Robert Connelly. Recruited and processed subjects in a
cross-sectional computerized study of mental imagery in adults, children, and teenagers.
June 1988 to March 1989.

MEMORIAL CHURCH, Harvard University, Cambridge, MA
Child Care Provider for children ages one to three during Sunday Services. Sept. 1988 to
May 1989.

RINDGE TEEN SHELTER, Department of Human Services, Cambridge, MA
Youth Coordinator. Staffed the shelter one night per week. Served as counselor and friend
to drop-in teenagers. Prepared weekly workshops on adolescent issues. Sept. 1988 to June
1989.

NATIONAL RED CROSS, Harvard University, Cambridge, MA
Blood Drive Coordinator. Established a student network to recruit blood donors.
Distributed information and publicity materials prior to Blood Drive. Served as volunteer
during the Drive. Sept. 1987 to May 1988.

ADDITIONAL SKILLS

Fully bilingual (Spanish/English) including translation experience.

ACTIVITIES

House Coordinator for Harvard House and Neighborhood Development Program, which
plans public service and community action programs in an effort to bring together Harvard
resources and the community. Interested in swimming, dance, and the application of
computers to education.

References Furnished Upon Request

Comments: Marta is interested in a teaching position. She planned her resume to
describe her extensive experience in youth work and community service. The
number of her activities and her responsible positions communicate her commitment, her energy, and her leadership experience. She lets the employer know that
she can provide references and will submit a detailed list of her coursework along
with her resume.

DIANE SIMMONS

North House F-16
Harvard College
Cambridge, MA   02138
(617) 555-3782

Permanent Address:
44 Spring Avenue
Princeton, NJ   05831
(201) 555-4353

EDUCATION

Harvard University, Cambridge, MA.   Candidate for 1991 B.A. honors degree in Women's Studies.   Coursework in history, modern and Shakespearean literature, French, psychology, music, and religion.   Agassiz Certificate of Merit for academic achievement of high distinction, 1987-88.   Harvard College Scholarship for academic achievement of high distinction, 1987-88.   Dean's List, 1987-88.

Ramaz Upper School, New York, NY.
National Merit Letter of Commendation, 1987.

WORK EXPERIENCE

Student Worker, Manuscripts Department of Schlesinger Library, Radcliffe College, Cambridge, MA.   Fall 1987 - present.

Salesperson, Hillside Farm, Truro, MA.
Family owned farmstand on Cape Cod.   Summers 1987, 1988.

Child care provider, for two-year old. Cambridge, MA. Spring 1988.

Salesperson, Eeyore's Books for Children, New York, NY.
Advised customers on age-appropriate children's literature. Spring 1987.

ACTIVITIES

Drama

"Anything Goes," Ramaz School, New York, NY, Spring 1987.
"Gymnasium," Ramaz School, Fall 1985.
"A Midsummer Night's Dream," Ramaz School, Spring 1985.
"The Me Nobody Knows," Summerstage, Dwight Englewood School,
     Englewood, NJ, Summer 1981.
"The Sound of Music," Players' Guild, Leonia, NJ, Summer 1980.

Writing

Writer, CUE Guide, Harvard College, Cambridge, MA.
Spring-Summer 1989.

Literary Editor and Writer, Yearbook, Ramaz School, New York, NY.
1985-87.

RESEARCH PROJECT

Schlesinger Library, Radcliffe College, Cambridge, MA.   Researched history and evolution of Women's Studies committee and concentration at Harvard-Radcliffe.   Spring 1988.

LANGUAGES: French, Hebrew.
TRAVEL: Israel, Scandinavia, England.

Comments: Diane is a senior applying for jobs in marketing, a field that requires creativity, strong writing skills, and interest in what motivates people. Diane gives very brief descriptions of her jobs in order to devote enough space for a full listing of her experiences in drama and writing. Note that her drama experience was in high school, but she has included it because an employer in marketing would be interested in that information.

JACOB K. BLIXEN

Present Address: Quincy 123   telephone: (617) 555-1234
                                    Harvard University
                                    Cambridge, MA 02138

Permanent Address: 11 Baxter Road   telephone: (617) 555-7654
                                    Lexington, MA 02173

EDUCATION   **Harvard University** candidate for 1991 B.A. honors degree in Applied Math — Decision and Control.

COURSEWORK: **Math and Physics:** Applied Algebra and Combinatorics, Differential Equations, Vector Space Theory, Mechanics, and Electro-magnetism.

                    Computer Science: Introduction to large-scale assembly code programming, Artificial Intelligence, Introduction to Computer Architecture, Theory of Computation.

                    Economics: Micro (including exposure to optimization techniques), Macro, and Statistics.

WORK EXPERIENCE — PROGRAMMING

TECHNICAL DATA CORPORATION, BOSTON, MA

Summer 85 and Summer 84   Analyzed sales and administrative functions. Recommended and instituted new operational procedures to aid in these tasks. Developed computer system to accomplish these goals and provided documentation and training to ensure implementation. System recorded sales activity, updated database, and supported user-defined ad hoc performance reports. System also serviced on-line queries. Designed software to accommodate future needs of this rapidly growing company. Summers 1990 and 1989.

POLAROID CORPORATION, CAMBRIDGE, MA

Summer 83   Formulated general and working specifications for **Engineering Change Notice Tracking System** to automate logging procedure and integrate micro and mainframe databases. Programmed application and wrote complete user and system documentation. Summer 1988.

Summer 82   Wrote working specifications and programmed **Joblist Control System** to computerize input and reporting of work performed in machine shop. System later copied and modified for several other applications at Polaroid. Also programmed **Inventory Control System** to provide information regarding acquisition and calibration of engineering equipment. Summer 1987.

OTHER WORK AND EXPERIENCE

September 82 - present   WHRB (Harvard Radio — a student-run, self-supporting, commercial station broadcasting to metropolitan Boston). Served on five-person station management board in 1990. Appointed news department co-director in 1989. Started as a reporter, and later became a day editor. Tasks included managing a staff of reporters and organizing a half-hour news show. September 1987 - present.

1979-82   Debate Team at Lexington High School, 1984-87. Team co-captain 1986-87.

INTERESTS   Bicycling, canoeing, and mountain climbing.

Comments: Jacob, a graduating senior, prominently lists his coursework in math and physics, computer science, and economics because it is directly related to the employment he seeks in software development. For emphasis, he lists his work experience in programming in a separate section and describes his accomplishments in these summer jobs. The selective use of boldface type in listing sections and subject areas and in the paragraphs under "Polaroid" is effective.

JOHN P. WHITE

College Address:
Eliot House 4B
Harvard University
Cambridge, MA 02138
(617) 555-6878

Permanent Address:
10 Cotton Road
Rumson, NJ 07760
(201) 555-1442

Education

HARVARD UNIVERSITY   Cambridge, MA
A.B. with honors degree in Government, expected in 1991. Harvard College Scholarship for academic achievement of high distinction. Dean's List. Electives in Statistics, Computer Science, Economics, and Game Theory. Worked 15 hours per week termtime to defray cost of tuition.

Work Experience

Research Analyst

KIDDER PEABODY   New York, NY
Interned in Corporate Finance and Litigation Research. Analyzed companies' financial and industry positions for valuation purposes. Organized private placement of stock. Co-wrote report on companies with more than one class of common stock. Supervised updating and revision of client transaction list. Summer 1990.

Equity Research Intern

FIDELITY INVESTMENTS   Boston, MA
Analyzed competitive position and market potential of the U.S. textile and apparel industry. Examined industry structure, export trends, and the implications of regulatory proposals on U.S. market share. Presented findings to senior management. Summer 1989.

Congressional Intern

SENATOR JOHN KERRY   Washington, DC
Researched nuclear energy and South African divestment. Drafted memos and participated in the speech writing for these issues. Summer 1988.

Workshop Coordinator

INSTITUTE OF POLITICS, JFK School of Government   Cambridge, MA
Coordinated undergraduate/graduate student workshops in Negotiation taught by Eileen Babbit of the Project on Negotiation at Harvard Law School. Termtime 1989.

Activities

Captain	Harvard Varsity Squash, All-Ivy
President	Harvard International Investment Club
Photographer	Harvard Crimson
Big Brother	Phillips Brooks House

Special Skills/Personal

Language   Spanish and French

Computer   Lotus 1-2-3, IBM Pagemaker, and MacIntosh

Travelled extensively in Europe, the Soviet Union, and Australia. Ragtime and Dixieland jazz pianist.

Comments: John is a senior interested in banking and finance. He designed his resume to emphasize his relevant work experience and his leadership abilities. Placing the job titles in the left margin for his work experience and in the center for his activities results in an attractive and effective format. Instead of using precious space to describe his student jobs, he states, "Worked 15 hours a week termtime..." in the education section.

James Whitcomb

Lowell Z-11   Permanent Address:
Harvard University   10 Cottage Lane
Cambridge, MA 02138   Minneapolis, MN 55416
(617) 555-1234   (612) 555-5678

EDUCATION

> Harvard University, Cambridge, MA. BA expected in June 1991 in
> English and American Literature. Significant coursework in Modern
> Literature and Poetry, Elizabethan Drama, Computer Systems, Mathemat-
> ics, and Medical Sciences. Dean's List.
>
> Phillips Academy, Andover, MA. Sept. 1985 - June 1987. Senior
> proctor of freshman dormitory; President, Cantata Choir; Orchestra;
> Jazz Band; Spring Musicals; National Merit Scholarship Commendation;
> Honor Roll.
>
> Madison West High School, Madison, WI. Sept. 1983 - June 1985.
> Drama, Musicals, Principal's Advisory Committee, Varsity Wrestling.
> High Honors.

ACTIVITIES

> Coxswain, Harvard University Lightweight and Heavyweight, Minnesota
> Boat Club and Phillips Academy Crews. Coached during practices,
> executed race strategy, steered shell, and "called" races.
> Achievements: Undefeated Collegiate racing record, 1988-90, including
> two Eastern Sprint Championships. Medal in Head of the Charles
> Regatta, 1988. Coached and raced with Minn. Boat club: won U.S.
> Nationals Senior Gold Medal and Elite Silver Medal; Canadian Henley
> Open Event Gold Medal, 1988.
>
> Filmmaking. Produced and acted in winning entry in Residential House
> Film Contest, Spring 1990. Current project: writing and directing
> original work, funded by the Harvard-Radcliffe Office for the Arts.

WORK EXPERIENCE

> Computer Programmer, University of Minnesota Department of Surgery.
> Wrote "artificial intelligence" data-checking programs and helped set
> up kidney transplant database. Summers 1986, 1987, 1988.
>
> Crew Instructor, Minnesota Boat Club. Taught novice crews; planned
> race strategies and preparation for experienced crews. Summers 1988,
> 1989, 1990.
>
> Lab Researcher, Institut Pasteur, Paris, France. Applied DNA Sequenc-
> ing and Plasmid Cloning techniques to Gene Regulation questions.
> Summer 1990.
>
> Lab Researcher, Harvard Medical School, Boston, MA. Applied Recombi-
> nant DNA and Gene Splicing techniques to Immunological questions.
> Fall 1989.

PERSONAL

> Skills: American Sign Language, CPR, PADI certified SCUBA;
> Computer Languages: Fortran, Pascal, COBOL, LISP, "C," BASIC.
>
> Interests: Piano, French Literature, Auto Mechanics, Squash.
>
> Travel: Western Europe, Venezuela.

Comments: James is seeking a position in private secondary schools. His resume communicates a breadth of interests, leadership experience, and success in competitions. In addition to teaching English, James would enjoy coaching crew or working with drama or film clubs. His skills in computer programming and familiarity with a number of different computer languages are likely to be valued by both faculty members and students.

NORA C. MASON

North House G-7
Harvard University
Cambridge, MA 02138
(617) 555-9876

6 Sand Street
Dedham, MA 02026
(617) 555-1234

EDUCATION

HARVARD UNIVERSITY   Cambridge, MA
A.B. in English and American Literature expected in June 1991. Honors candidate. Agassiz Award for High
Academic Achievement. Additional coursework in Economics, Statistics, Management, Business, Fine Arts, and
Popular Culture.

MILTON ACADEMY   Milton, MA
Class of 1987. Captain, Varsity Track; Varsity Field hockey; Business and Advertising Manager of Yearbook; Vice-
President of Admissions Tour Guide Program.

ADVERTISING AND PUBLIC RELATIONS EXPERIENCE

CAMBRIDGE COMMUNITY SERVICES   Cambridge, MA
Public Relations Intern for TeenWork Program. Wrote press releases. Designed and distributed photo displays.
Planned, organized, and secured funding for TeenWork events. Wrote student/employer case studies for use in
1991 funding proposals. Summer 1990.

HARVARD MAGAZINE   Cambridge, MA
Advertising Intern. Sold classified advertising. Managed accounts receivable. Assisted in designing and
completing seasonal advertising campaigns. Developed sales and word processing skills. Summer 1990.

WGBH-TV CHANNEL 2   Allston, MA
Commercial Marketing Intern. Previewed programs under market consideration and assisted in writing reviews.
Answered inquiries regarding programming and commercial distribution of Public Television programs. Spring
1990.

KENYON AND ECKHARDT   Boston, MA
Advertising Intern. Assisted Account Executive with daily business activities. Observed strategy meetings and
progress of a particular account. Interviewed Senior Vice-President and General Manager for Business and
Management course term paper. Fall 1989.

HILL HOLLIDAY CONNORS COSMOPULOS INC.   Boston, MA
Administrative Assistant. Planned, organized, and allocated expenses for catered meals for client meetings and
company parties. Organized print advertisements in mechanical library. Exposure to all departments and current
business prospects. Summer 1988.

OTHER WORK EXPERIENCE

HARVARD BUSINESS SCHOOL, CAREER RESOURCE CENTER   Boston, MA
Assist students with company and industry research for career planning. Prepare company and industry informational packages from current periodicals. 1989-present.

BANK OF BOSTON   Boston, MA
Research Library Assistant. Prepared briefing package for the Strategic Planning department's trip to Far East.
Responsible for updating international files. Executed computer searches on industry trends for Loan Officers.
Summer 1989.

ACTIVITIES AND INTERESTS

Institute of Politics study group on Television News, Peer Counseling, dance, running, writing.

Comments: Nora targeted her resume for advertising and public relations. To
emphasize her extensive career-related experience, she devoted the entire center
section to advertising and placed her other work experience in a separate section
below.

LAURA WEBSTER

Present Address:
47 Mt. Vernon Street
Cambridge, MA 02140
(617) 555-3456

Permanent Address:
RD 2 - Box 1
Stowe, VT 05672
(802) 555-4567

EDUCATION

BREADLOAF SCHOOL OF ENGLISH, Middlebury College. M.A. in English expected August 1991.

HARVARD-RADCLIFFE COLLEGE. B.A. Cum Laude in Anthropology. Harvard College Scholarship for academic achievement of high distinction, 1984-85. Elected Captain of Varsity Ice Hockey for three consecutive years. Winner Joseph D. Bertagna Award (for leadership and dedication), 1985.

WORK EXPERIENCE

JOINT VOLUNTARY AGENCY   BANGKOK, THAILAND
Caseworker. Interviewed Lao refugees seeking asylum in the United States to establish their status under current immigration policy. Prepared refugee files for presentation to U.S. Immigration and Naturalization Service for final decisions. Worked in refugee camps and in Bangkok headquarters. (October-November 1988).

THE TAFT SCHOOL   WATERTOWN, CT
English Teacher/Admissions Officer. Taught two sections of ninth graders. Interviewed and evaluated candidates for admission. Advised students from A Better Chance, Inc. (national program serving minority youth). Coached Varsity Ice Hockey and Field Hockey. Supervised senior dormitory. (September 1986 - June 1988).

THE MADEIRA SCHOOL   GREENWAY, VA
Assistant Director of Admissions/Dorm Adult. Interviewed and evaluated candidates for admission. Traveled extensively throughout continental U.S. for recruiting purposes. Supervised forty-member dormitory. (July 1985 - July 1986).

TRAVEL EXPERIENCE

SOUTHEAST ASIA - SOUTH PACIFIC. Traveled independently for nine months. Activities included bicycling in China and Tasmania, trekking in Nepal, helping on a New Zealand sheep farm, and working with Lao refugees. (September 1988 - June 1989).

EUROPE. Have visited most major countries. Worked as an au-pair girl for American family in Italy. (June - July 1981).

KENYA. Participant in "Operation Crossroads Africa." Worked on construction of elementary school. (June - August 1983). Participant in "The Experiment in International Living." Worked on irrigation project. (June - August 1980).

PERSONAL

Interests include running (successfully completed 1986 Boston Marathon), reading, and writing. Proficient in French. Studied Swahili for one year.

Comments: After three years in education and a year of travel and volunteer service abroad, Laura is exploring career opportunities in international development. She gives equal emphasis to both her work and travel, because the intercultural aspects of these experiences would be valued for positions in international development.

JEFFREY R. MARSHALL
220 East Street
Gardner, MA 01840
508/555-2356

EXPERIENCE

3/90 - present   GARDNER CABLEVISION   Gardner, MA
General Manager
Managed staff of 24 serving 20,000 customers. 450mHz cable system with
Impulse Pay per view.
*Restructured management team, replaced three.
*Managed beta test of Newtek technology.

1/88 - 3/90   ABC CABLE TELEVISION   Wayne, PA
General Manager
Managed three clustered cable systems serving 10,000+ customers in six
communities.
*Reversed union sentiment in 15-member staff.
*Increased customer base 3%, Pay penetration 12.6%.
*Increased $2,000,000 revenue by 6%.
*Improved operating cash flow 6%.
*Won national sales contest.

8/84 - 8/88   REGIONAL CABLESYSTEMS   Easton, IN
Regional Business Manager
Managed cash flow and assets for nine cable television systems. Prepared long-
range plans, annual budgets, and quarterly forecast.
*Increased operating cash flow $1,200,000.
*Improved pretax profit 25%.

5/82 - 9/83   MINNEAPOLIS CABLE   Minneapolis, MN
Auditor
Audited cable television systems. Traveled 70%.
*Audited 20 systems; 1,000 to 100,000+ customers.
*Identified $100,000 pole attachment savings.

1/81 - 3/83   GULF OIL COMPANY   Springfield, IL
Budget/Planning Analyst
Administered financial and analytical services to two retail sales districts with
functional responsibility for seven people.
*Implemented automated maintenance program, saving $64,000.

EDUCATION   HARVARD UNIVERSITY   Cambridge, MA
9/76 - 6/80   Bachelor of Arts in Economics. Earned varsity letter in heavyweight crew.

OTHER   COMMUNITY SERVICE
Rotary Club of Wayne Sergeant at Arms
Wayne United Way Commercial Chairman
Junior Achievement Advisor: West Pennsylvania Top Company

LANGUAGE
Proficient in oral and written French.

Comments: Jeffrey has eight years of experience in the cable TV industry. His
current objective is to secure a management position with greater responsibility in
cable TV or in related media corporations. He has designed his resume to document
his steady advancement in the industry, highlighting the description of his achievements in each position through the use of asterisks.

ANDREW ROBERT PARKS

Winthrop 92
Harvard University
Cambridge, MA 02138
(617) 555-8910

45 Elmhurst Dr.
Florence, AL 45036
(205) 555-8765

EDUCATION

HARVARD UNIVERSITY. Honors candidate for A.B. degree in Social Studies, expected June 1991. Senior thesis: "The Roman Catholic Church and Democratic Development in Haiti." Additional coursework in economics, psychology, and religion.

TABB HIGH SCHOOL, Florence, AL. Diploma 1986. National Honor Society. National Merit Scholarship Finalist. Class Forensics Award.

COMMUNITY SERVICE

VICE PRESIDENT   CATHOLIC STUDENT ASSOCIATION OF HARVARD-RADCLIFFE
Coordinated the activities of six committees. Organized social events. Co-chairperson of the Social Justice Committee. Organized and conducted weekly construction and repair projects at homeless shelters in Boston. Served soup, bread, and conversation to homeless people in Cambridge. Organized and conducted 24-hour ecumenical prayer vigil for peace and justice, Fall 1986-Spring 1991.

PASTORAL AIDE   FOND-DES-BLACS, HAITI
Taught English and worked in a medical dispensary, January-June 1989. Researched senior thesis, June-August 1990.

TUTOR AND COOK   PHILLIPS BROOKS HOUSE, HARVARD UNIVERSITY
Tutored prisoners for general equivalency diplomas. Tutored a Haitian high school student in English as a second language. Cooked for and served 25 or more homeless people in Cambridge once a week, Fall 1986-Spring 1990.

MAINTENANCE PERSON   MOUNTAIN CHRISTIAN ACADEMY, MARTIN, KY
Performed maintenance duties at a private school for underprivileged children and participated in other community building activities, September-December 1988.

MANAGEMENT

HEAD TEACHER   MEMORIAL CHURCH OF HARVARD-RADCLIFFE
Designed curriculum and liturgy, directed pageants, and taught children from age 4 to 9, Fall 1990 to Spring 1991. Provided day care for children age 3 and under, Fall 1989-Spring 1990.

STUDENT CAPTAIN   STUDENT PORTER PROGRAM, HARVARD UNIVERSITY
Supervised the clean-up of a residential house with over 100 rooms, June of 1987,1988, and 1990. Reunion liquor caterer and bell hop, June of 1987,1988, and 1990. Janitor, Fall 1986-Spring 1991.

SUMMER EMPLOYMENT

STOCKPERSON   MERCEDES-BENZ, HAMPTON, VA
Supplied the assembly line with parts, 1988 and 1989.

PARKING LOT ATTENDANT   BUSCH GARDENS, WILLIAMSBURG, VA
Conducted 5000 cars daily into and out of the lots, 1987.

ADDITIONAL SKILLS AND INTERESTS

French, Haitian Creole, word processing, forklift driving, creative writing, rowing, swimming, dancing, folk music, travelling.

Comments: Andrew is a senior interested in a position with a public service organization such as Catholic Relief Services. Using a functional/chronological format, he emphasizes his extensive experience in community service and management through college activities and student jobs, only briefly mentioning his summer jobs.

ELIZABETH MARTELL
54 Appian Way • Cambridge, MA 02138 • (H) 617/555-0123 • (W) 617/555-3210

EDUCATION

Harvard College Cambridge, MA. A.B. English and American Literature and Language. Focus on 19th Century Anglo-American Literature. Other courses in children's literature, child development, Australian history and literature, Shakespeare and drama. (1985-1989)

Cate School Carpinteria, CA. Robert Frost Poetry Award, 1985; faculty-selected dorm monitor, 1984-1985; Scholarship Award, 1984; Cate Chorale; Cate Counterpoints (select female a cappella group); editorial board of school literary magazine; student librarian; Los Niños (public service in Mexico). (1983-1985)

Exeter Union High School Exeter, CA. California Scholarship Federation, 1981-1983; Varsity swim team, 1981-1983 (lettered 1981); Swimming All-League Award, 1982. (1981-1983)

TEACHING EXPERIENCE

Instructor Buckingham, Browne & Nichols Summer School, Lower Camp (ages 3-5), Cambridge, MA. Organized crafts and outdoor activities for group of 15 pre-kindergartners. Taught swimming. Supervised assistant teacher. (Summers 1988, 1989)

Instructor/Lifeguard Malkin Athletic Center, Harvard University. Taught weekly private swim lessons. Taught swimming and CPR to college affiliates. Lifeguard at college pool. (1987-1989)

Counselor Harvard Alumni Association, 25th Reunion Committee. Served as counselor to children of alumni (ages 6-12). (June 1986, 1988)

Instructor/Proctor Exploration Summer Program, Intermediate level (grades 7-9), Wellesley, MA. Developed and taught courses in weaving and writing mystery stories. Planned and conducted sports and arts activities. Proctored girls' dormitory. Led tours in Boston and New England. (Summer 1987)

ADMINISTRATIVE EXPERIENCE

Administrative Assistant Office of Human Resources, Harvard University. Supervise hiring and scheduling of 25 student employees. Provide administrative and financial support: editing, statistics, word processing, data entry, accounts payable and receivable. Manage office purchasing. Instruct and direct clients to resources. Schedule appointments. (September 1989-present)

Coordinator One-to-One Program, Phillips Brooks House, Harvard University. Interviewed college and youth candidates for big sibling program. Arranged informational meetings and group discussions for program members. Volunteered as big sister to pre-teenage girl. (1986-1988)

SKILLS

Drama Performed in *Suite Dreams*, 1987; *A Streetcar Named Desire*, 1987; and *Picnic*, 1988. Served as properties mistress for *The Merry Wives of Windsor*, 1988, and as costumer for *How to Succeed in Business*, 1985, and for *Inherit the Wind*, 1989. Worked on set construction and studied theater.

Arts & Crafts Able to give guidance and instruction in marionettes, puppets, cross stitch, sewing, weaving, tie dye, papier mâché, drawing, and painting.

Writing Pursue poetry and short story writing. Studied creative writing in high school and college.

Certifications American Red Cross: WSI-NM, ALS, Basic Water Safety, Emergency Water Safety, CPR-Community, CPRI-Community, BLS, BLSI, Standard First Aid and First Responder.

Comments: Elizabeth is a recent alumna interested in teaching. Listing both her high schools, one private and one public, shows the breadth of her school experience. By creating a "Teaching Experience" section, she highlights her summer and termtime teaching positions and her experience working with young people. The "Skills" section provides her with the opportunity to list explicitly the curricular and extracurricular areas in which she is prepared to work with students.

SUZANNE M. LILLY
103 Commonwealth Avenue
Boston, MA 02122
H - (617) 555-1234   W - (617) 555-5678

EDUCATION

HARVARD UNIVERSITY Ph.D. expected October 1992 in Biology. Dissertation on the dynamics of Eskimo hunting in a multi-prey system. Mathematical models and multivariate statistical techniques are used to examine causes of variation in harvest levels of wildlife populations.

M.SC. in Zoology, University of British Columbia, 1983. Thesis on population dynamics of marmots.

B.SC. in Biology (Honors), University of Victoria, Canada, 1978.

PROFESSIONAL EXPERIENCE

STATISTICAL CONSULTANT, Marttila and Kiley, Boston, April-May 1991. Recommended statistical techniques for analysis of political polls.

TEACHING FELLOW, Harvard University and University of British Columbia Biology Departments. 1990.

DIRECTOR OF RESEARCH, Baffin Region Inuit Association, Northwest Territories, Canada. 1984 to 1989.
Designed and managed the first successful survey of wildlife harvest levels in the Northwest Territories. Raised over $1,000,000 to fund the project. Through public meetings, persuaded 99% of Eskimo hunters in the eastern arctic to participate in the survey. Managed budget and designed accounting system. Hired and supervised a staff of 20. Statistically analyzed a 3 million piece data set using custom computer programs.

PROJECT MANAGER, Consultant to Northwest Territories Wildlife Service. 1983-1984.
Assessed the impact of construction of a highway on wildlife populations. First in N.W.T. to implement a statistical model to estimate numbers of moose not observed during aerial surveys.

WILDLIFE BIOLOGIST, Northwest Territories Wildlife Service. 1982-1983.
Conducted research on population dynamics of polar bears, caribou, seals, and falcons. Published government reports with management recommendations.

SKILLS

Analytical ability: Accounting, computer programming, statistics.
Developed a system for predicting point spread in National Football League games. Scored in top 1% in Graduate Record Exam.
Language training: Spanish, French, Latin, Inukitut (Eskimo)
Communication skills: scientific papers, successful funding proposals, political analyst for CBC radio

CITIZENSHIP: Dual U.S.-Canadian

Comments: Suzanne is applying for positions in investment banking. She has planned her resume to commmunicate her familiarity with statistical analysis. She describes her administrative and supervisory experience as Director of Research and communicates an adventurous spirit and breadth of interests. Her dual citizenship is important information for a potential employer.

JOSHUA KLEITMAN

Center for International Affairs
Harvard University
1737 Cambridge Street
Cambridge, MA 02138
(617) 555-6543

Home Address:
13 Parkvale Ave
Allston, MA 02134
(617) 555-4321

Education

HARVARD UNIVERSITY. Ph.D. expected June 1991, Department of Government. A number of courses in domestic and international economics, international business. 1984-Present.

HARVARD UNIVERSITY. M.A., Government, 1990.

BRANDEIS UNIVERSITY. B.A., Politics, 1983.

Experience

Strategic/Organizational Analysis
DISSERTATION: "Soviet Strategic Culture and the Postwar Formation of Doctrine for Europe." Analyzed the organizational structure and professional culture of the Soviet military in order to identify strengths and weaknesses in Soviet strategy and force planning. Developed proposals for defeating the Soviets' strategy in war, and for conducting successful arms control negotiations. 1986-Present.

Teaching
TEACHING FELLOW, Department of Government, Harvard University. Designed and taught two seminars for honors candidates on special topics in international politics. Supervised thesis research of senior honors students. 1986-Present.

TUTOR in Government, Adams House, Harvard University. Taught introductory seminar in American politics to sophomores. Advised students on their academic programs. 1987-1989.

Administration
CHAIRMAN, Board of Trustees, Park Place Condominium. Administer a 24-unit condominium and an annual budget of $93,000. Facilitated transition to self-management; negotiated a dispute with developer over unfinished work in the condominium. Directed search for new management company and negotiated contract with same. 1989-Present.

CHAIRMAN, MacArthur Fellows in International Security, Harvard University. Schedule, organize and chair meetings and seminars of a group of graduate students. Report on group's activities to the University Committee on International Security. 1989-Present.

Activities

SENIOR EDITOR and Graduate Advisor, *The Salient*, a journal of political commentary, Harvard College. Assisted in founding journal, advised editorial board on editorial policy, contributed articles regularly. 1986-1988.

FOUNDER, editor and manager of *The Intelligentsia*, a journal of humor and political satire, Brandeis University. With one other student, founded journal; recruited volunteer staff; raised working capital and managed finances, including supervision of sales and ad marketing; set editorial policy and assigned articles; wrote and edited articles. 1980-1983.

Academic Awards and Fellowships

MacArthur Fellowship in International Security
Hubert H. Humphrey Fellowship in Arms Control and Disarmament Studies, U.S. Arms Control
　　Disarmament Agency
National Science Foundation Graduate Fellowship
Phi Beta Kappa

Comments: Joshua is seeking a position in policy analysis in the public or private sector. He describes his experiences under three skill areas which are relevant to this field. The placement of his dissertation under experiences provides the opportunity to emphasize "Strategic/Organizational Analysis" as a skill area. The capitalized job titles highlight his intitiative and leadership qualities.

WILLIAM B. ALDRIDGE

Center for International Affairs
Harvard University
1737 Cambridge Street
Cambridge, MA 02138
(617) 555-8765

Home Address:
44 Whitney Street
Arlington, MA 02174
(617) 555-3456

EDUCATION   Ph.D. University of North Carolina, Chapel Hill, (1991, expected).
  Field: Political Science. Dissertation: "International Economic Negotiation:
  Spain, France and the Enlargement of the European Community, 1977-1985."
  M.A. University of North Carolina, Chapel Hill, 1987.
  Field: Political Science. Thesis: "The Politics of Direct Foreign Investment in
  Mexico: The Case of U.S. Food-Processing Companies, 1977-1982."
  B.A. with Highest Honors, University of North Carolina, Chapel Hill, 1982.
  Major: Political Science and Economics. Phi Beta Kappa.

WORK EXPERIENCE

Business   **Small Businessman,** 1988-present.
  Established a small business to represent Caves Andre Guenet, a French wine
  company. Conducted a marketing study, organized wine tastings, and promoted their products at wine shows. Sold 3,000 cases of wine to importers.

Consulting   **Consultant,** UNESCO's Division of Science and Technology Policies, Paris, 1986.
  Researched science and technology policies of the industrialized countries.
  Prepared a 50-page report.

Administration   **Chairman,** Commission on Graduate and Professional Student Education,
  University of North Carolina, Chapel Hill, 1988-89.
  Conceived and initiated a computer-assisted study of graduate professional
  student education. Designed the questionnaire and headed the team
  responsible for conducting the survey and compiling the data.

  Assistant to the Director of the Mexican Fellowship Program, University of
  North Carolina, Chapel Hill, 1982-83.
  Coordinated the program's activities. Organized the orientation sessions and
  planned several field trips.

Teaching   **Teaching Fellow in Political Science,** University of North Carolina, Chapel
  Hill, 1986, 1988, 1988-89.
  Taught seven sections of courses in international relations and European
  politics.

FELLOWSHIPS   Ford Foundation Predoctoral Fellowship, Harvard University, Center for
  International Affairs, 1990-91. Chateaubriand Fellowship, Paris, 1989-90.
  Fulbright Fellowship, Mexico, 1986-87. Rotary Foundation Fellowship, Paris,
  1983-84.

LANGUAGES   Fluent in French and Spanish.

TRAVEL   Lived in France and Mexico. Traveled extensively in Western Europe.
  Biked 3,500 miles from Kentucky to Oregon.

Comments: William is interested in a position in international consulting or
finance. His list of areas of experience in the left margin alerts the reader
immediately to the range of his background. He includes the titles of his Ph.D.
dissertation and his M.A. thesis because they are both research topics relevant to this
job search. The resume communicates high energy, entrepreneurial spirit, and
extensive international experience.

CARLA M. BOWMAN
14 Eastman Avenue
Arlington, MA 02143
(617) 555-0934

CAREER OBJECTIVE

Employment in the broad field of student life using social work skills and other significant experience.

EDUCATION

University of Michigan, Ann Arbor, M.S.W, 1985, School of Social Work.
Program included two one-year internships and coursework in research and evaluation, social policy and planning, and interpersonal practice.
Purdue University, Lafayette, IN, B.A. 1967
Major in English Literature, Minor in Psychology.

SIGNIFICANT EMPLOYMENT AND VOLUNTEER EXPERIENCE

Interviewing and Counseling
* Counseled adolescent individuals, groups, and their families in innovative social welfare agency.
* Cooperated on a team of professionals serving battered women and children.
* Interviewed human service professionals about their agency's response to basic human needs.
* Interviewed mental health clients to assess human rights in community housing.

Coordinating
* Managed office and aided Executive Director of Planned Parenthood Federation of America, Inc. Coordinated clinical volunteers and staff.
* Held vice-presidency of Silver Spring, MD, League of Women Voters, 1979-1983.
* Coordinated College and Career Fair, Silver Spring High, 1979-1983.
* Helped organize and maintain the Silver Spring Parents Coalition for Youth.
* Organized Silver Spring, MD neighborhood organization around park and recreational issues.

Writing
* Co-authored research paper on teenage mothers' postpartum rate of return to school.
* Constructed surveys for Silver Spring League of Women Voters and Silver Spring Central School Development Office.
* Coordinated and wrote study on Basic Human Needs for Maryland League of Women Voters.
* Contributed chapter to *Women in Crisis*, Stonewood Press, 1987.

Fundraising
* Worked in campaigns for local political candidates in Maryland, Michigan, and Massachusetts.
* Helped raise increasing amounts of money through various parent-sponsored projects in public and private schools in Maryland, Michigan, and Massachusetts.
* Set up Education Fund for League of Women Voters of Silver Spring.

EMPLOYERS

Simmons College, Boston, MA (1989-Present)
Harvard Square Business Association, Cambridge, MA (1985-1988)
Women's Crisis Center of Ann Arbor, Ann Arbor, MI (1984-85)
Child and Family Service of Washtenaw County, Ann Arbor, MI (1983-84)
Planned Parenthood Federation of America, Inc., Washington, DC (1967-1973)

Comments: Carla has many years of work experience. In order to focus the reader on the skills that she has to offer for employment in student services, she has chosen a functional format. She lists her education at the top because her M.S.W. is relevant to her career objective. In the main part of the resume, she organizes descriptions of her work experience into four categories. At the bottom she lists her employers, but chooses not to give her job titles.

F. ROBERTO GARCIA

420 Illinois Avenue
Chicago, IL 60734

Home: (312) 555-9876
Work: (312) 555-5678

QUALIFYING EXPERIENCE	Over eleven years in banking, trade, and economics. Specialized in lending to the High Technology industry with in-depth knowledge of the computer sector. Supervised line and staff positions in commercial banking activities in Brazil and Chile. Prepared annual budget and developed credit and marketing strategy. Established Credit Administration department to supervise lending activities and interact with Head Office audit teams. Active in promoting private sector development efforts: Chairman of the American Chamber of Commerce Economics Committee in Chile (1988-89); compiled annual economic and trade assessment report distributed to the private sector and professional organizations.

EMPLOYMENT

1980 - Present   **CONTINENTAL BANK, NATIONAL ASSOCIATION, Chicago, Illinois**

1990 - Present   **VICE PRESIDENT, HIGH TECHNOLOGY DIVISION, Chicago**
Senior lending officer in specialized lending group focusing on high technology firms in the Midwest. Marketing and credit responsibility for corporate customers with $200 million in credit facilities. Evaluate clients' businesses, industries, and markets. Prepare and present credit proposals to Credit Committee. Cross-sell bank services including cash management, foreign exchange, leasing, corporate trust, and shareholder services.

Financed client's $17 million corporate headquarters expansion.
Negotiated and executed a $100 million revolving/term loan agreement.
Set up multicurrency credit facilities overseas for customer.
Worked on lending team which recently refinanced Upjohn Laboratories, Inc.'s $350 million facility.

1985 - 1989   **VICE PRESIDENT, SANTIAGO BRANCH, Chile**
Senior Credit Officer responsible for all credit and marketing functions. Hired and trained lending officers and reviewed their performance.

Increased number of multinational accounts, doubled non-interest income, and converted department into the most profitable division.
Designed and implemented management information system to track bank earnings from each individual client.
Introduced strict Loan Review process reducing problem loan portfolio from $15 to $1 million.

1982 - 1984   **ASSISTANT MANAGER, SAO PAULO BRANCH, Brazil**
Voting member of the Credit and Loan Review Committees. Regional Manager coordinating credit and marketing activities.

1980 - 1981   **MANAGEMENT TRAINEE, LOAN OFFICER DEVELOPMENT PROGRAM, Chicago**
Completed the bank's commercial lending training program. Received award for outstanding contribution in Chicago Chamber of Commerce Membership Drive.

EDUCATION

1975 - 1979   **HARVARD COLLEGE, Cambridge, Massachusetts**
A.B. cum laude in Economics.

LANGUAGES   Completely fluent in English, Spanish, and Portuguese. Working knowledge of French.

PERSONAL   U.S. citizen. Lived 15 years in Spain and Portugal. Traveled extensively in Europe, Latin America, and the United States. Three children. Excellent health. Willing to travel and be posted overseas.

Comments: Roberto wishes to return to a position in international banking. He has developed a statement of "Qualifying Experience" to give the reader a summary of his banking experience. In the "Employment" section he first describes his responsibilities for each of his positions, then lists his accomplishments to highlight his expertise. He places his education at the bottom of the resume, along with his language skills. He volunteers personal information about his health, family, and willingness to travel or live overseas.

WRITING LETTERS

There are four kinds of letters you will be writing: letters requesting a career advisory interview, letters inquiring about employment opportunities, letters applying for a job, and follow-up letters.

The letters you write to career advisers and to employers are an opportunity to present yourself and to initiate or reinforce a relationship. In career exploration and job-hunting letters, your objective is to motivate the recipient to invite you for an interview. In follow-up letters, your objective is to say thank you, to express interest in a continuing relationship, and to structure the next step.

Letters are personal communications from you to another individual. Within the constraints of expected form and style, you should express your individuality. The appearance, the form, the style, and the content of the letter all contribute to the messages you convey and influence the evaluation and response of the reader.

Appearance. Each letter should be addressed to an individual, printed or typed on plain paper with a matching envelope. If you are enclosing a resume, the letter and the resume should be done on matching bond paper. Most business correspondence is done on white paper with black type, but ecru paper is also acceptable. Do not use erasable bond paper; it smudges and adheres to other papers. Letters should have absolutely no errors: no typos, no misspelled words, no noticeable corrections. If you are not a good typist, enlist the help of a friend or pay a typing or word processing service to produce your letters. If you have access to a word processor, you can produce personalized error-free letters more efficiently.

Form. Each letter should be short, fitting easily on one page with generous margins on all sides. Paragraphs should be limited to four to eight lines whenever possible, because business letters are usually scanned quickly. The first line of each paragraph is the most important. As you work on drafts of letters, try reading only the first lines of each paragraph to see what information is communicated.

Your name and address should be typed on the letter. Standard business form, with your address and the date at the top right, the addressee's name and address at the left just above the salutation, is preferable. At the end of the letter, your full name may be typed below your signature or at the top right with the address.

Letters should be addressed to an individual by name, with correct title and address. Titles should be used in the salutation if appropriate, such as "Dear Dr. Carley," "Dear Judge O'Neil," but in most correspondence the salutation will be "Dear Mr. Smith," "Dear Ms. White." First names should not be used unless you are personally acquainted with the addressee. It is advisable to try to find out whether a woman prefers to be addressed as "Miss," "Mrs.," or "Ms.," but if her preference is not known, "Ms." is acceptable.

Style. The style you use in your letters expresses your individuality and your personality. To show respect for the reader's time, you want to be forthright, informative, and concise. Business letters are not supposed to have the flow of smooth literary prose, but should be written to communicate information with clarity and impact. Simple direct sentences are usually preferable. Within these constraints, there is a great deal of latitude for personal choice in sentence structure and choice of words.

The following descriptions and samples of career exploration letters, job-hunting letters, and follow-up letters are meant to be helpful suggestions and models. Your letters should be personal communications to the individual you are addressing, saying what you want to say as clearly and directly as possible.

Career Exploration Letters

A letter requesting an interview for career advice should engage the interest of the reader in you and in your quest for knowledge about his career field. You are asking a busy person to spend a little time discussing his career experiences and his perspectives on career development with you. Your letter should give enough information about you and about why you selected the addressee as a potential career adviser to make him want to meet with you.

In the first paragraph, it is usual to identify yourself and request an interview. If you were referred to the person by a mutual friend, you should mention the friend's name in the first sentence. If you obtained his name in another way, mention how you selected him as a potential career adviser. Try to limit the first paragraph to three or four lines.

In one of the middle paragraphs, describe the basis of your interest in that career field and why you would value the opportunity for an information interview. You might make reference to some related reading you have done. In this paragraph you want to make clear why this person can be particularly helpful to you in your career search.

In another paragraph, you should talk about yourself. If you are enclosing a resume, this paragraph can discuss work qualifications and skills or expand on academic work and experience related to that career field. If you are not enclosing a resume, use this paragraph to present a brief personal introduction to your experiences. In general, you will want to enclose a resume, although you may prefer to introduce yourself in the letter and share your resume when you meet for an interview.

The closing paragraph must make clear what the next step is. Usually it is best to state when you will be available for an interview and that you will call to arrange a mutually convenient time. This way you save the career adviser the time and expense of writing you a letter. If the career adviser is far away, however, you may have to rely on his responding by mail.

Employment Inquiry Letters

As you clarify the kind of job you would like or the kind of organization for which you would like to work, it is important that you identify potential employers and write to them. Your letter should be addressed to the top executive of an organization or to a department head who has the power to hire you.

This cover letter is similar to a career exploration letter in that you are requesting advice, but now you are seeking job-hunting advice and very specific information about entry-level jobs and career pathways in that organization or similar organizations. The introductory sentence should arouse the reader's interest in you. If you have a personal referral or any kind of link with the potential employer, be sure that you state it prominently.

In the middle paragraphs, you should make it evident that you are knowledgeable about the company and the industry. In a separate paragraph, highlight and expand on information in your resume that is particularly relevant to this career field. Make clear why you think you are well qualified for this type of work. In the closing paragraph, express your interest in seeking advice from this person, and state that you will call at some specific time in the near future, usually in about a week, to arrange a mutually convenient time for an interview. You are writing to a busy executive; save him the time and expense of responding by letter.

Job Application Letters

Never send a resume alone when applying for a job. Whether you hear about the job opening from a friend, read about it in the newspaper or a magazine, or find it in campus job listings, learn as much as you can about the employer and the job and use this information to develop a cover letter.

The objective of the cover letter is to impress the employer with your qualifications, motivation, and interest in the job so that he will want to interview you. The first paragraph should identify clearly what job you are applying for and why you are interested in the job. If a mutual friend recommended that you apply for the job, mention his name.

In the middle paragraphs, discuss your qualifications for the job, expanding on experiences described on the resume; make clear your knowledge and interest in the organization and in the particular job; describe specific accomplishments as documentation of the skills and work characteristics you would bring to the job. How you divide this into two or three paragraphs will depend on your content and what you want to emphasize. Sometimes a paragraph on relevant work experience and one on academic experience makes sense. Sometimes a paragraph on why you want this particular job and on why you are qualified is most appropriate. Remember, your lead sentences should state important information succinctly and your paragraphs should be only four to eight lines long.

In the closing paragraph, express your interest in meeting with the employer to discuss the requirements of the job and your qualifications. If you have not heard from the employer within a reasonable amount of time (perhaps a week or two), telephone the individual to whom you addressed your letter to find out how the job search is progressing. This will communicate your continued interest in the position and may lead to an interview.

Follow-Up Letters

Every person with whom you have interviews while you are exploring careers or job hunting may become a friend, adviser, or mentor if you keep in touch. After every interview, you should write to thank the person. If it was a career exploration meeting, you might discuss briefly how the interview was helpful to you, or recount further reflections you have had on questions which were discussed. If the person gave you names to contact, let him know if you will be seeing those people. If the person gave you specific suggestions or advice on your job hunt, report back on the effectiveness of that advice. Be sure to thank the person for his time and assistance.

If this was an employment interview, you should express your interest in the job. Incorporating information you learned during the interview, you should restate briefly your special qualifications for the job and your interest in the organization.

Follow-up letters should be short, should say thank you, and, if the interview was an enjoyable one, should state interest in a continuing relationship.

When you have accepted a job, you should share your good news by writing a brief note to all the people who assisted you in your career exploration and job hunting. Maintaining these relationships can be rewarding and helpful in unexpected ways.

The following sample letters and comments illustrate some of the principles of letter writing. They should help you formulate your requests for career advice and conduct an effective job search.

Career Exploration Letter 1

Quincy House 621
Harvard University
Cambridge, MA 02138
February 28, 1991

Mr. John Roden
Vice President
Smith and O'Hare, Inc.
83 Park Avenue
New York, NY 10021

Dear Mr. Roden,

I would like to meet with you to discuss careers in public relations when I am visiting in New York during spring vacation. I am seeking information about what public relations firms do and how a liberal arts graduate can qualify for employment in the field.

I am a junior at Harvard majoring in philosophy. I feel that a career that demands creativity and involves writing would be an ideal match for me. In my extracurricular activities, I usually assume the responsibility for publicity. I enjoy thinking of ways to publicize events: making posters, writing ads for the newspaper, and thinking up new gimmicks to attract attention to a specific event.

I will call you next week in hope of arranging to meet with you in your office on Thursday, March 28, or Friday, March 29.

Sincerely,

Deborah Kent

Comments: Direct and explicit, Deborah shows she has given some thought to the characteristics and skills required for public relations.

Career Exploration Letter 2

35 Irving Street
Cambridge, MA 02138
November 5, 1990

Mr. Norman Walters
Commercial Lending Officer
Chemical Bank
315 Wall Street
New York, NY 10172

Dear Mr. Walters,

I have just completed my Ph.D. in English and am interested in learning about careers in commercial banking. I selected your name from the Career Advisory File because you earned a Ph.D. in history.

I have an appointment this year as an instructor in expository writing, but I am devoting as much time as I can to exploring nonacademic careers.

Banking is a career option that I have been reading and thinking about for some time. I would like to visit you at Chemical Bank to talk about your work. Your impressions of the challenges and satisfactions of your banking career as compared with those found in an academic career would be of great interest to me. In addition, I would like to learn more about the ways in which your graduate training prepared you for a banking career.

I will call you next week to see if I can arrange a mutually convenient time to meet with you on November 15 or 16, when I will be in New York.

Sincerely,

William Clark

Comments: Although this lead sentence might not be appropriate in a letter to a non-Ph.D., in this case it identifies a common history with Mr. Walters, who has been in banking for only two years. William makes explicit that, by taking an appointment as an instructor, he has arranged time for his career exploration and job hunt.

Career Exploration Letter 3

Currier House
Harvard University
Cambridge, MA 02138
May 3, 1991

Ms. Doreen Snyder
Research Director
Foreign Policy Institute
1300 Pennsylvania Avenue
Washington, DC 20006

Dear Ms. Snyder,

I read with interest your article in an issue of Foreign Policy and would like to have the opportunity to meet with you to discuss careers in international relations.

Currently I am a junior at Harvard and am concentrating in government. For my senior honors thesis, I am conducting a study of United States policy toward Vietnam during the 1950s.

I have a strong interest in working in international relations and would like to discuss with you the career opportunities and entry-level jobs. Your advice on graduate study would also be greatly appreciated.

I will be in Washington during June to research some primary source materials for my thesis. I will call you when I arrive to see if there is a convenient time when I might come to talk with you.

Sincerely,

George Coulter

Comments: Doreen Snyder is not a career adviser, so George states in the first paragraph how he identified her. Mention of his senior thesis topic indicates he is developing background in foreign policy research.

Career Exploration Letter 4

26 Winthrop Street
Cambridge, MA 02138
July 5, 1991

Mr. Clarence Duggan
Vice President of Marketing
McArdle Industries
101 Princeton Street
Philadelphia, PA 19105

Dear Mr. Duggan,

Mr. Malcolm Battle suggested that I write to you because of my interest in learning about the consumer products industry and most especially about the marketing of consumer products.

From my reading and from conversation with Mr. Battle, I have become excited about the data analysis and creative planning that go into developing marketing strategy. It sounds challenging and fascinating to me.

I have a strong quantitative background from academic work in sociology. I have done several projects that require compilation and analysis of demographic data. Now I am looking for opportunities to apply these skills in business.

I will be in Philadelphia at the end of July and will call next week to see if I may visit you to talk about careers in marketing.

Sincerely,

Martha Sullivan

Comments: Martha decided not to mention in this letter that she has completed a Ph.D., but she will discuss that with Mr. Duggan during the interview. She indicates that she has some knowledge of marketing already, which should make a positive impression on Mr. Duggan.

Employment Inquiry Letter 1

5104 Crawford, N.W.
Washington, DC   20008
February 25, 1991

Ms.Joan Meyer
Principal
Washington Cathedral Elementary School
3500 Crowley Road, N.W.
Washington, DC 20016

Dear Ms. Meyer,

Writing and biology became my academic loves in high school, and they remain my strongest academic interests today. Now, as a Harvard graduate, I seek the chance to teach writing and biology.

I enjoy young people. I feel comfortable with the subjects I hope to teach. I work with energy and enthusiasm, patience and persistence. Through my work with college students and young children, I have learned how to listen, how to encourage learning, and how to respect a person's efforts. Through my teaching, I have learned the value of feedback, the constructive uses of discipline, and the need for guidelines and limits.

I know that the Washington Cathedral School places great value on both the academic growth of students and their personal development. I share that commitment. I want to participate actively in your school community as a teacher and as an advisor for extracurricular activities such as journalism, wildflower identification, and quilting.

I will provide additional references, an official transcript, or other information upon request. I would like to visit your school and have the opportunity to meet you. I look forward to hearing from you and hope that I can join your school community this fall.

Sincerely,

Rona Shore

Enc: Resume and Course List

Comments: The first sentence attracts attention and draws the reader into the letter. The letter communicates the enthusiasm and diversity of interests that headmasters look for. Rona realized that this letter would be evaluated as a sample of her writing ability. She makes a special effort to make it interesting.

Employment Inquiry Letter 2

Peabody Terrace #1234
Cambridge, MA 02138
August 24, 1991

Mr. Arnold Q. Bass
President, International Division
Chesebrough-Ponds, Inc.
33 Benedict Place
Greenwich, CT 06830

Dear Mr. Bass,

I am writing to you because I would like to explore opportunities at Chesebrough-Ponds International Division in marketing and public relations for Latin America.

I have majored in Latin American Studies and have lived in Costa Rica. For my senior honors thesis, I did a comparative study of the role of the Catholic church in Mexico and Costa Rica. Awarded a research grant by my department, I spent one month in Mexico City and one month in San Jose interviewing residents and priests in various parishes. I learned a great deal about the role of the church in their lives.

After graduation, I returned to Costa Rica to teach in a Catholic high school in the community where I had done my research. This gave me the opportunity to become completely fluent in Spanish and knowledgeable about the local culture and mores. I became interested in people's reactions to imported consumer goods in the marketplace.

I am intrigued with the challenge of marketing consumer products in a different culture. Although these consumers have some needs and desires similar to ours, their priorities and preferences are different. Consequently, a different marketing approach is appropriate.

I would like the chance to talk with you about international marketing with Chesebrough-Ponds. I will call you next week to arrange a time for us to meet.

Sincerely,

Charles Ramos

Comments: As a result of his career research, Charles has identified an employer and a function to which he brings some special insights. His letter is direct and informative.

Employment Inquiry Letter 3

One Holland Street
Dedham, MA 02345
December 3, 1990

Kevin Seeley
WKOR Radio
4568 Cherry Street
Brookline, MA 02147

Dear Mr. Seeley,

If you're looking for a young, spirited, eager, interested, and conscientious worker to help in any way possible around the station, I'm for you.

I've recently graduated from Harvard College with a deep love for music, choral music in particular. Although I have no hands-on experience with radio as a medium, I'm a quick learner and very motivated to gain the skills necessary to succeed in this field.

I would be honored to meet you. If you could spare a moment of your time to discuss employment or general advice on careers in broadcasting with me, please give me a call at (617) 555-2459. I'm looking forward to hearing from you.

Sincerely,

Joanne F. Highland

Comments: Joanne designed the upbeat letter to catch the attention of a busy radio personality. She is forthright about her lack of experience and makes it clear that she would appreciate any opportunity to gain experience in the broadcasting field. Her statement, "I would be honored to meet you," flatters the recipient, recognizing that he is a celebrity.

Employment Inquiry Letter 4

77 Monroe Street
Batavia, NY 14321
January 4, 1991

Mr. Joseph Burton
Executive Vice President
Second National Bank of Boston
100 Federal Street
Boston, MA 02110

Dear Mr. Burton,

I am seeking a position in international banking. I believe my experience in cross-cultural communication and my quantitative skills would be useful to the international operations of the Second National Bank of Boston.

I am a specialist on Canada. I have designed and conducted surveys of Canadian executives in the automotive and computer industries on their views toward Canadian-American economic integration. For the past two years I have been researching government-owned corporations involved in energy and regional economic development. Because these corporations play an increasingly important role in the Canadian economy and because several borrow on international capital markets, it has become clear to me that they constitute an important market segment for any bank with Canadian interests.

I have traveled extensively throughout Canada, have lived in Ottawa, and am actively involved in the University of Windsor's International Business Studies Research Unit. In November I will be attending the University's conference on changes in North American banking.

I have also traveled and pursued research in Europe and Africa. I have been affiliated with Harvard's Center for International Affairs as a research associate and as a workshop manager responsible for the center's conference on international political economy. I have expertise in statistics and the computer analysis of data using software packages.

I want to learn about career opportunities in international banking. I would come to Boston to meet with you at your convenience.

Sincerely,

James A. Sullivan

Enclosure

Comments: This is a strong letter. James tells Mr. Burton what motivates him to write, and what he has to offer the bank. It is an interesting example of the discussion of transferable knowledge and skills.

Job Application Letter 1

24 Oxford Street
Harvard University
Cambridge, MA 02138
March 11, 1991

Mr. Timothy Borden, Personnel Officer
USGS National Center, MS-215
U.S. Geological Survey
12201 Sunrise Valley Drive
Reston, VA 22092

Dear Mr. Borden,

I am writing to apply for the position of geologist at USGS Headquarters as announced on the Career America College Hotline.

As you can see from the enclosed resume and SF171, I am a senior concentrating in earth and planetary sciences at Harvard University. My studies and research in the past four years have focused on geochemistry, particularly as it relates to the late-stage magmatic processes and to the petrology of meteorites. Through my research and work experience during college, I have become proficient in the use of a variety of laboratory equipment, such as the electron microprobe and the scanning electron microscope.

The position of geologist would allow me to utilize my geological knowledge to define and solve problems. I would find this very exciting and challenging.

In addition, I enjoy both creative and technical writing, as well as editing, and take pleasure in designing presentations of technical material.

I will be in the Washington, D.C. area for the week beginning March 25. I would like very much to meet with you at that time to discuss my candidacy for this position.

Sincerely,

Catherine A. Pointer

Comments: In applying for this technical position, Catherine describes her subject interests and her familiarity with laboratory equipment. She also communicates her writing and presentation skills in a way that conveys enthusiasm and confidence.

Job Application Letter 2

52 Linnaean Street
Cambridge, MA 02138
May 10, 1991

Mr. James L. Freer, President
Cambridge Consulting Group
60 Brattle Street
Cambridge, MA 02138

Dear Mr. Freer,

I am writing to apply to be a research associate at Cambridge Consulting Group. I expect to receive my bachelor's degree from Harvard in June, with honors in history and science.

I enjoy doing research and have experience with quantitative methods. My senior honors thesis, an historical study of the development of antibiotics, provided me the invaluable experience of planning and conducting a large research project. My wholehearted efforts in both the research and the writing of the thesis were rewarded with a magna plus.

In my course in computer programming, I was required to write programs to solve eight out of ten different problems; I enjoyed the challenge of using the computer to devise solutions to problems and I actually solved all ten! I look forward to an opportunity to increase my proficiency in computer use.

I will call you next week to see when we might meet to talk about this position.

Sincerely,

Marjorie Matson

Comments: To make clear her qualifications for this job, Marjorie describes her research and computer programming experience and documents her level of competence in these areas. She also communicates enthusiasm and high energy.

Job Application Letter 3

4 Chauncy Street
Cambridge, MA 02138
March 4, 1991

Mr. Stephen McCarthy
Creative Services Department
Young and Rubicam, Inc.
285 Madison Avenue
New York, NY 10017

Dear Mr. McCarthy,

I'm the new kid on the advertising block. I may look strange at first, but I think you're going to like me. Here's why:

I have experience using words and pictures in public communications. In 1986 I wrote the guide to the "Images of Labor" exhibit at the National Museum of American History in Washington, D.C.

I have an extremely flexible writing style. I have written technical reports for hospital administrators and union officials and recently presented a thesis to the most intellectually demanding history department in the nation.

I know how to sell ideas. As a teaching fellow at Harvard, I developed audiovisual presentations and dramatized historical events in order to promote enthusiasm about the past. And when all else failed, my sense of humor proved to be an ace in the hole.

I have enclosed two writing samples for your perusal. The first consists of the sketches I wrote for the National Museum's art exhibit. These have since been published in Moe Foner, ed., Images of Labor (New York: Pilgrim Press, 1987). The second is a chapter of my thesis, a dramatic reconstruction of a riot which occurred more than one hundred years ago.

I am a person who writes simply and succinctly, who enjoys working with people, and who prefers to make history rather than simply write about it. This is why I am interested in becoming an advertising copywriter.

I would like to meet with you to talk about the copywriting position at Young and Rubicam as advertised in Adweek. I will call next week to find out when that might be possible.

Sincerely,

Adam Devereaux

Comments: This letter is appropriate for the advertising field. Adam sells his writing ability through this letter and the writing samples which he attaches. The uniqueness of the letter illustrates his creativity.

Follow-Up Letter 1

44 East 67th Street
New York, NY 10021
December 28, 1991

Ms. Sally Weston
Account Executive
Raines, Kelly, and Jenkins
90 Madison Avenue
New York, NY 10016

Dear Ms. Weston,

Thank you for meeting with me yesterday to talk about careers in advertising. Our conversation has made me more eager than ever to become a part of this exciting world. I have called your friend Cynthia Dorman and plan to meet with her tomorrow.

I appreciate your candor in suggesting ways to improve my resume. When I return to Harvard, I will write to the agencies you suggested, enclosing my "new and improved" resume, and requesting interviews during intersession. I will keep you informed on the progress of my job hunt.

Thank you for your helpful advice and encouraging support.

Sincerely,

Jan Schmidt

Comments: In this excellent follow-up letter, Jan reports what she is doing about Ms. Weston's advice and recommendations. She has laid the groundwork for what could prove to be a continuing supportive relationship.

Follow-Up Letter 2

46 Linnaean Street
Cambridge, MA 02138
April 22, 1991

Mr. Robert Marshall
Belmont Valley School
4 Village Hill Road
Belmont, MA 02178

Dear Mr. Marshall,

Thank you for sharing with me some of your experiences in teaching. It is clear that young people are important to you. I am sure your students feel your concern.

I had not visited a high school classroom since I was a student myself. It was very different watching you teach and imagining myself in your place.

I will be program director at Camp Tahoe this summer. When I return to Cambridge in the fall, I will get in touch with you.

Sincerely,

Gerald Fox

Comments: Gerald communicates that he enjoyed his visit. He gives news of his summer plans and tells Mr. Marshall when he will be in touch with him, letting him know that he wishes to continue their relationship.

Follow-Up Letter 3

216 Kirkland Street, Apt. 2
Cambridge, MA 02138
August 2, 1987

Ms. Madeline Jencks
City Advertising Agency
76 Madison Avenue
New York, NY 10020

Dear Ms. Jencks,

I am writing to tell you my good news. I have just taken a job as account executive trainee at Rowes Advertising Agency. I am very pleased to have this opportunity to begin my career in advertising.

I have applied for many jobs and interviewed with many people in advertising and public relations since last March. During these months I have often reflected on my conversation with you and some of the questions you raised. Your sharing with me the satisfactions you had found in your career influenced me to seek a job in advertising.

I will keep you informed of my progress. I hope we can have lunch sometime after I finish my training program.

Thank you for your advice and continuing support.

Sincerely,

John F. Sellars

Comments: John is writing to thank all the people who helped him during his job hunt and to let them know where he will be working. Keeping his career advisers informed about his career progress demonstrates his thoughtfulness and will help him build friendships with professionals in his field.

REQUESTING LETTERS OF RECOMMENDATION

Whom to Ask

The best people to write letters of recommendation for you are professors, instructors, employers, and advisers who have supervised and evaluated work of which you are proud. It is important that the person know you well. If you keep in touch with your favorite teachers and employers over the years and share with them the development of your plans, they will enjoy having the opportunity to write letters that may assist you in progressing toward your goals.

If the letter of recommendation that you are requesting is for a specific purpose, you should identify potential letter writers who have had the opportunity to observe you developing and utilizing skills and talents which will be valued in that selection process. You will almost always want an academic reference written by a professor or a tutor who can describe your approach to learning, your analytic and problem-solving abilities, and your written and oral communication skills. You may also want a letter from a person who can comment on other personal strengths, leadership skills, interpersonal skills, and work characteristics such as initiative, attention to detail, and high standards of performance. It is most helpful if they are familiar with and can describe specific examples. All letter writers should address your potential for success in the given field.

As you complete a course, an extracurricular activity, or employment in which you are pleased with your achievement, you may want to request a general letter of recommendation from your professor, supervisor, or employer. If you find it difficult or awkward to request letters, remember that anyone who teaches or supervises the work of others expects to be asked to serve as a reference. The advantage of requesting a letter at the time you complete the course or the job is that your performance is fresh in the mind of the letter writer, and therefore he can speak specifically about your accomplishments. There is also the advantage that you are in contact with the potential letter writer, whereas later on you might have difficulty finding him. Sometime in the future, you may want to ask writers of general letters of recommendation to rewrite their letters for a specific purpose. This is not a burdensome task for the writer. The major effort is the development of the first letter of recommendation about you; future editions require very little time.

How to Ask

Because you want letters that are positive and supportive, you should always give the person the opportunity to tell you if he does not think he is the best person to write for you, or that he does not know you well enough, or that he is too busy.

The best way to ask for a letter of recommendation is in a personal conference when you have the opportunity to discuss your reason for requesting the letter of recommendation. If you share with the letter writer your goals and aspirations, and the reasons why you are making the particular application you are asking him to support, it will assist him in writing about you as you see yourself.

If it is not possible to meet with the person, the choice between making your request by telephone or by letter depends upon your relationship with the person. It is a choice based on what you feel is the best substitute for the personal conference.

What Information to Provide

It is important that you think through carefully what information will be helpful to the person who is writing a letter for you. It is important to refresh the letter writer's memory of the work that you have done for him. If some time has passed since you completed this work, you may want to supply materials such as the research paper you wrote or the special project that you did. You may also want to give a progress report on relevant experiences since that time.

For a letter of reference for a specific application, you should supply the letter writer with information about the criteria used in the selection process. This will provide the opportunity to speak to the qualities in which the selection committee is most interested.

The other kind of information you want to supply is information about yourself. A copy of your resume, your transcript, and a draft of your application essay will assist the writer in viewing you and speaking of you in a broader context.

The Deadline

Be sure to inform your letter writer of the deadline for the receipt of letters of recommendation. Request your letter two to four weeks ahead of the deadline, if possible. It is important to provide a stamped, addressed envelope for the letter and a written note stating to whom the letter should be addressed and the deadline.

Remember that your letter writers have many other responsibilities to fulfill and other deadlines to meet. It is perfectly acceptable to follow up a few days before the deadline to be sure that your letter of recommendation has been sent or to make certain it has been received. Meeting the deadline is your responsibility.

Confidentiality

Since the enactment of the Buckley Amendment in 1974 a person has the legal right to read letters of recommendation written about him unless he waives that right.

Some recipients consider a confidential letter to be a more honest and accurate appraisal of a candidate; in fact, you may find that confidential letters are strongly preferred in some cases. However, you may want to read your letters in order to select which letters to use for a particular purpose, depending on which of your qualities are discussed.

The issue of whether or not to waive your right to read your letters is complicated. It is your decision to make. You may find it helpful to discuss your options with your career counselor or academic adviser.

INTERVIEWING FOR JOBS

An interview is a conversation with a purpose. You, the interviewee, share the responsibility for making the interview productive. The interview provides you the opportunity to convince the employer that you are the best candidate for the job he must fill. You can be helpful to the employer by answering the following questions:

Can you do the job? Do you have the skills or can you learn the skills to do this job? What in your past experience is relevant to predicting that you can learn to do this job?

Do you want to do this job? Are you highly motivated to do this job well? How does this job fit into your long-range goals? Will you invest your best effort toward high achievement in this job?

Will you fit in? Will you work well with other team members whose work is related to yours? Will you be productive?

If you have researched the job and the organization as discussed in Chapter 3, you should be able to discuss these questions effectively. You can select from your past achievements those that most clearly document that you can fulfill the responsibilities of this position and that you will fit in well in this organization.

There are some general characteristics that employers seek. They want employees who are energetic, enthusiastic, responsible, and thoughtful of others. They want employees who approach new situations with confidence, who learn quickly, and who are willing to take initiative. They want employees who communicate clearly, who listen carefully, who express themselves concisely, and who are precise and honest. All of these qualities can be demonstrated in the interview. The information exchanged in an interview is not all verbalized. Your appearance, your manner, your voice, your total presence, communicate aspects of your qualifications and suitability for the job. Your behavior in the interview is taken as a brief sample of how you will conduct yourself on the job.

Types of Interviews

The first interview for a job is often a screening interview and may be conducted on campus. The second interview or interviews are usually conducted on site by the supervisors and perhaps by potential colleagues. Sometimes you will be interviewed over lunch, and sometimes you will be interviewed in a group. It is helpful to think about the objectives of each of these types of interviews.

The purpose of the **screening interview** is to screen out applicants who are not qualified and to select the applicants who would seem to be the best prospects for making a contribution to the organization. Emphasis is placed on whether you will be compatible with people in the organization. This is a subjective judgement made by the interviewer based on how much he enjoyed meeting and conversing with you. The interviewer also makes a judgement about how interested you are in his organization. To demonstrate your interest, you need to have researched the organization and be able to converse knowledgeably about it.

The **second interview** or interviews are usually held in the place of employment and constitute your opportunity to meet the supervisor and colleagues with whom you will be working. Any information that you can learn ahead of time about these people will be helpful to you. In these interviews, the interviewers are trying to decide if you are the best qualified person of all those whom they are interviewing. Each person that you meet and talk with will be asked to evaluate your suitability for this job.

The **lunch interview** is usually programmed to be a more personal and informal interview than the others, and is often held with potential peers rather than with supervisors. Remember that those who take you to lunch will also be asked to evaluate your candidacy. It is not advisable to engage in conversation about intimate personal matters or controversial subjects. If you are asked personal questions which you prefer not to answer, it is best to pass them over lightly and respond with a question in a different subject. Probably the best kind of conversation is one about mutual interests. It is perfectly acceptable to use this opportunity to ask why these people enjoy working for this organization and to try to gain some insight into what work would be like for you on this job. It is usually best not to have a drink at lunch and not to order a meal that is difficult and messy to eat.

Sometimes you will be given a **group interview** with other candidates present. This is a difficult kind of interview because your behavior in relation to the other candidates as well as your behavior toward the interviewer is being evaluated. You will have to judge how aggressive or outspoken you should be. It is probably best to demonstrate in this situation that you are a good team member; that you have good ideas and can ask good questions; that you listen to others; and that you think about and respond to their contributions. Even when the stated purpose of the group meeting is to give you information about the organization, your behavior is being observed.

Another type of interview is the **board interview**, where you are the only candidate present and you are being interviewed by several people. This is a very challenging kind of interview because you will be trying to respond accurately and appropriately to four or five individuals. The best approach is usually to focus on the person asking the question while the question is being asked, so that you can be thinking through the best response. While you are making your response, your attention will be primarily on the questioner, but you should look around to see whether you have the attention and support of other members of the interviewing group. When you go into a group interview, it is particularly important that you try to have some knowledge of the names, positions, and backgrounds of each of the interviewers.

Styles of Interviews

In general there are four different interviewing styles: directive, nondirective, stress, and unplanned.

In the **directive interview**, the interviewer will ask you questions. He may be asking exactly the same questions of every candidate. You should answer each question with the most relevant information you can select. You should keep your answers short and concise. To learn how well you think on your feet, the interviewer may outline a problem and ask you how you would solve it. Before the interview ends, the interviewer will probably ask you if you have any questions, and you should make sure that you have a question at that time.

The **nondirective interview** will start with an open-ended question such as "Tell me about yourself." This is not an invitation to relate your life history, but it gives you the opportunity to tell the interviewer why you are qualified for the job. Even though the opening is a very comprehensive one, you should not make a long response, but should attempt to initiate a conversation. Keep any answer limited to about two to three minutes in length. Start with a few observations about what you think the job requires and why you think you can do it, then ask the interviewer what he thinks is most important about the job. Usually the nondirective interviewer is seeking a more informal exchange and will be glad to respond to your questions throughout the interview.

In **stress interviews**, the interviewer will ask you questions which are very difficult to answer or which have no answer. He is intentionally putting you under pressure to test whether you are able to control your emotions and retain your composure. The answer that you give is not important so long as you stay calm. Another type of question which puts you under stress is the one posed by the interviewer who asks you to take a position on a certain issue and then disagrees with the position you have taken. In this case it is best to defend your position, but moderately, so that you show strength of conviction but not unwillingness to consider other positions. Stress interviews are not used very commonly, but may be appropriate when the job is one which requires you to perform under stress.

The fourth kind of interview is the **unplanned interview** by the inexperienced interviewer. This interviewer will seem to be uncomfortable with his role as interviewer. Your objective should be to help make him comfortable and to give him the information which he will need to make hiring decisions. You will need to take the initiative with such an interviewer, but that does not mean you should conduct a monologue. Try to develop a conversation which gives you the opportunity to communicate your qualifications, but which also gives the interviewer the opportunity to participate.

Preparing for Interviews

Get as much information ahead of time as you can about the job, about the organization, and about the interviewer. Organizations are unique; you want to understand the personality of this particular one so that you can tailor your presentation. The interview only gives time for the employer to get a glimpse of you. Be sure that the glimpse includes the kind of information about you that he needs in order to feel confident that you are the best candidate for the job.

How you prepare for an interview depends on your work style. For some people, writing out answers to questions that they expect to be asked is helpful, but if this would lead you to memorize answers and deliver them by rote, it will be counterproductive. Some people outline or list the points they want to make about why they want the job and what they have to offer. Some people find it helpful to practice with a friend or with an adviser, responding to questions such as those listed later in this chapter.

Video interview training is very helpful because it gives you the opportunity to observe your interview behavior as well as hear your responses to questions. Some campus career services offer video interview training sessions.

General Outline of an Interview

The impression that you make as you enter the interviewing room is lasting. Your attire should be appropriate for the job for which you are applying. Your stance and stride should express confidence. Your handshake, eye contact, and self-introduction, "I'm Jane Smith," should express energy, enthusiasm, and anticipation.

Usually the interviewer will open the interview, introducing informal conversation about a mutual interest, the weather, or some topic which he hopes will make you feel at ease. This opening conversation will give you some indication of the style of interview that you are going to have. This part of the interview is very much like the kind of conversation that takes place between any two people who have just been introduced to each other.

In the main body of the interview, the interviewer is responsible for the format or style of the interview. Usually he will initiate the substantive part of the interview with a question, but if you find the opening stretching out, it is acceptable to initiate conversation about your qualifications for the job. You should adapt your behavior in the interview to the interviewer's style and pace. Listen carefully to his questions and respond with the most pertinent, relevant information you can, taking a moment to organize your thoughts, if necessary.

The content of the interview is mostly up to you. Remember that the employer wants to get to know you. He wants to understand your work values and your career aspirations. It is not your past experiences per se that are important, but how you approached each opportunity, what you accomplished, and how you reflect on what you learned from the experience. If you convince him that you put forth your best effort in academic or nonacademic responsibilities in the past, he will assume that you are ready to make that kind of commitment to your work in his organization.

Many employers ask what you think you will be doing in five or ten years. Don't be misled by this question! They do not expect you to name a job title and income level in their own organization. They want to know whether you have given thought to your future and what kinds of aspirations you have. It is appropriate to be quite general in your response, but to communicate that you look forward to advancing in your field.

Your objective is to make the interview a shared conversation, so it is perfectly all right to complete your response with a question for the interviewer. For example, if the interviewer started the interview with the question "Tell me about yourself," you might respond with a brief statement of how you became interested in the job and why you think you will enjoy it, and conclude with a question to the interviewer about the job.

Usually the interviewer will take responsibility for closing the interview. He will probably give you some evaluation of the interview, and he should most certainly outline what the next step will be. If the interviewer does not offer you information about how the job search is being conducted and when you can expect to hear from the organization about another interview or about the final selection, it is appropriate for you to ask for this information before concluding the interview. Ideally, the interview will have been a conversation that both have enjoyed, and you will conclude by telling each other so.

It is important that you follow up the interview with a thank-you note. (See the "Writing Letters" section.) This gives you the opportunity to express, once again, your interest in the job, and perhaps to comment briefly on a topic in the interview that you felt was incompletely covered or a question that was raised but was not answered by you at that time. Your thank-you note should be brief.

Questions Frequently Asked by Employers

The following is just a sampling of questions that you might be asked. If you think about how you will answer these questions to give the employer the information he needs about you, you will be prepared for most interviews.

- What is the accomplishment of which you are most proud?
- What do you see yourself doing five years from now? Ten years from now?
- Why do you think you are qualified for this position?
- Tell me about yourself.
- What are your special strengths and weaknesses?
- What will you do if you don't get this job?
- Why did you study for a Ph.D. in History?
- Why did you concentrate in Romance languages?
- What did you learn from (some experience on resume)?
- Why did you compete to write for your campus newspaper?
- Did playing varsity football help prepare you for your future career?

- Can you work under pressure, with deadlines?
- Do you prefer working with others or by yourself?
- Do you like work with (younger) (older) people?
- Why have you chosen a career in (whatever)?
- Do you plan to go to graduate school?
- What would be your ideal job?
- Why are you changing careers?
- How do you think your degree in liberal arts can help you in this job?
- Why are you interested in our firm?

You might also be asked how you would handle a hypothetical situation that you might encounter in the position for which you are a candidate.

Questions You Might Want to Ask the Interviewer

You already have experience in asking employers questions about careers from your career exploration interviews. The difference in questions you might ask in a job interview is that they should be pertinent to the job in question and should make evident that you have researched the employer.

Here are a few examples:

- What qualifications do you think are most important for this job?
- What are the career opportunities in this organization for people who start in this position?
- How are job assignments decided at the end of the training program?
- What would be my position twelve months from now?
- I read in *Newsweek* that your company is having difficulty in European markets. Was this article accurate? How is your company responding?
- Into what markets does the company expect to expand?
- I read in *Fortune* that the newly appointed vice-presidents are all people who have been promoted within the organization. Is this a tradition in this company?
- Your organization has many prominent individuals on its board of trustees. Do you think this accounts for your fundraising and programming success?

Responding to Illegal or Inappropriate Questions

Federal regulations prohibit employment interviewers from asking questions about age, race, religion, ethnic origin, or arrest record (asking about convictions is legal, but not about arrests). In most states there are regulations against asking about marital status, family, day care arrangements, or spouse's career unless the information relates to performance of the job. Women are more likely than men to be asked about these personal matters.

Before you start interviewing, you should decide how you plan to respond to questions about your personal life. You can state that you think the question is not job-related and refuse to answer it. You can respond, "I'm not sure I understand the intent of your question." You can make a noncommittal reply and ask a question that returns the conversation to a job-related topic. You can answer the question, giving information about your personal life. If you are interested in a job, the third option is probably most likely to result in a positive interview.

Some examples of nonanswers are:

Are you interested in marriage and children? Right now I am interested in getting started in my career. I have always thought I would marry, but if I do, it will be later. (Return to some previous topic, for instance: What are the opportunities for advancement with your firm?)

Do you have a girlfriend/boyfriend? I have close friends whose company I enjoy. If you hire me for this job and I move to New York, I am sure I will develop new friendships there.

Who will take care of your children while you are at work? I have made arrangements for the care of my children and am prepared to fulfill the responsibilities of my job. Who would my supervisor be in this position?

You should be able to think of responses which make clear to the interviewer without embarrassing him that you are not going to answer illegal questions or engage in personal conversation with him. If the interviewer returns repeatedly to inappropriate topics, you may want to end the interview.

After the interview, you will want to assess whether the illegal questions or inappropriate questions are symptomatic of company policies to which you object. If you feel the employer does not observe fair employment practices, you probably will not want to work for him. If the interviewer persisted in asking illegal questions, you may want to explore whether you have grounds for filing a legal complaint.

Good Luck!

Every interview is a unique adventure. Be prepared to be responsive and spontaneous.

Be yourself at your professional best. Present those aspects of yourself which best meet the employer's needs.

Act confident, not cocky. That will help you feel confident.

Listen carefully. Be sure you understand a question before you answer.

Ask perceptive questions. When reading company literature, prepare questions that will show you have thought analytically about the company's current status or future direction

Let your enthusiasm show. Being professional does not require cool restraint. Be friendly and responsive. These are qualities that will be expected of you once you are on the job.

EVALUATING JOB OFFERS

Well, you've done it! Your search has been successful, and you have a job offer in hand. Naturally, you are excited and would like to accept it. Chances are that you will do exactly that, but before you do, there are some questions you should ask yourself.

- Is this job right for you?
- Are you waiting to hear from other prospective employers?
- Do you have strong negative feelings about any aspect of the job or the organization?
- Is the salary acceptable?

The time to answer these questions is before you make a commitment, not after you are on the job.

Is This the Right Job for You?

Naturally, you were selective about which positions you applied for in the first place. During your research, you screened out those which did not appeal to you or which were unsuitable for one reason or another. The employment interview provided you with a firsthand glimpse of the employer and gave you the opportunity to ask questions that you deemed important. It is likely that you would not have continued as a candidate if there were serious points of disagreement or if certain features of the job were totally unacceptable to you. Now that you have been offered the job, however, you want to evaluate carefully all the information you can learn about the position and the company.

Ask yourself some of the same questions you asked as you began your career exploration.

- Will this job challenge you to develop your abilities and learn new skills?
- Is the work interesting and worthwhile?
- Do you like the work environment?
- Do you like the people?
- Is there opportunity for advancement in the job?
- Is the organization one with which you would like to be associated?
- Is the geographic location one in which you want to live?
- Are the benefits (health insurance, vacation, and the like) adequate?
- Is the salary acceptable?

Your positive answers to these questions should outnumber your negative ones. Although it is not possible to get everything you want in your first job, it should be a position in which you can feel challenged and one that provides opportunity to learn.

How Much Should You Expect to Be Paid?

Salary will probably figure in your deliberations. You will need to make a certain amount of money to support yourself, to pay off educational debts you may have accumulated, to afford some of your favorite leisure activities, and to set aside a bit for those inevitable unforeseen expenses which are a part of life. Of course, you will need to have realistic expectations in terms of lifestyle. On the income from your first job, you cannot expect to be able to afford the housing, leisure activities, wardrobe, vacations, family that you dream about having someday. It is the salary expectation over time that you want to take into consideration.

Your personal needs and desires have little influence on the salary a prospective employer offers you. He will offer what he has determined is a fair price based on the industry, the organization's internal structure and salary schedule, the geographic location, your qualifications and experience, and what he perceives to be your potential value to the organization. With so many variables and with so many factors assessed by the employer, how do you evaluate the fairness of an offer? You do what you have been doing from the start of your career exploration—research, research, research!

Where Do You Get Salary Information?

You are already familiar with resources that can give you some idea of what salary to expect. The *Occupational Outlook Handbook, The American Almanac of Jobs and Salaries,* and other career books give approximate salary ranges. The professional journals you have been reading are likely to publish articles or studies on compensation in their respective fields. Professional associations often conduct surveys of their members and might provide some information about salary ranges. The help wanted ads in newspapers and journals will sometimes list ranges for positions similar to the one you are considering, in a variety of geographic locations. All of these publications give you information about salaries.

Do remember, however, that the size of the organization can make a big difference. Large organizations may pay slightly more, but have comparatively rigid salary scales and performance review schedules; small employers may reward outstanding performance more readily with bonuses and pay increases, but may not offer the same employee benefits as a large employer. Because of the differences from firm to firm, and industry to industry, your personal contacts can be a good source of information, either about salaries within their respective firms, or within a particular industry or profession. Your career advisers will probably know the approximate salary schedules of their competitors. It is important to remember during your investigation that you are seeking an equitable range, not a definite figure.

When Do You Raise the Money Question?

As a rule, salary is one of the last items to be discussed, if it is at all, in the interviewing phase of job hunting. This usually works to your advantage, because you will have had an opportunity to demonstrate your potential value to the employer. Sometimes salary is mentioned only when a job offer is made; other times it is one of the first items on an interviewer's agenda. In any case, you should be thinking about what is an acceptable range to you. That way you will be prepared when the discussion of salary takes place.

If you are offered a position over the telephone, express your pleasure at receiving the offer and your positive interest in the organization. The next step should be either that you receive a letter detailing the offer and giving specifics of the job description, salary, and benefits as appropriate, or that you have a conference with the employer to discuss such specifics. If the employer does not tell you which to expect, you should ask. A job offer should be confirmed in writing or in personal conference.

It is acceptable to ask for time to make your decision. If you are expecting to hear from other employers, you may want to inform them that you have received an offer. Perhaps they will be able to give you information about when they will reach their own decision.

Do not accept a job offer unless you are ready to commit yourself to that employer. When you accept a job offer, you should withdraw your name from all other competitions. Employers within an industry or field communicate with one another, and your reneging on the acceptance of one job to take another may damage your reputation throughout the industry or field.

MANAGING YOUR FIRST DAYS ON THE JOB

Starting a new job is an exciting adventure. There is a great deal to learn. Every organization has its own customs, priorities, and rewards; every supervisor is a unique individual. Your first days are a time for observing, listening, reading, asking questions, seeking guidance, and getting to know your fellow workers.

Learning the Corporate Culture

Every organization has its own culture consisting of value systems, recognition systems, expected behavior patterns, and formal and informal communication networks.

In strong culture companies, the value system is expressed by the company slogan: "THINK," "Progress Is Our Most Important Product," "Better Things for Better Living Through Chemistry." Whether explicitly stated in a slogan or personified by "company heroes," the values of an organization guide the decisions of managers, influence the behavior of the workers, and determine the reward system.

Individuals selected for special recognition because they have demonstrated outstanding achievement in a valued activity are sometimes referred to as "company heroes." Recognition may or may not include promotion, but it is always public; for example, the "Programmer of the Month" or membership in the "100% Club." Observing who gets recognized and for what accomplishments gives you insight into the organization's values.

Expected behavior patterns are often expressed as "the way we do things around here." Styles of interaction and procedures for getting things done are usually best learned by observation. You will probably find that almost everyone around you is willing to help you learn, if you ask. It is wiser to ask for advice on procedures than to plunge ahead and damage your working relationships by inappropriate behavior.

The informal communication network provides "insider information" and interpretations of official decisions and events in the organization. To get plugged into the informal channels of communication, you need only be a good listener. If you do a lot of listening and resist expressing opinions during your first days, you will gain a great deal of insight into the organization, and you will learn who are reliable sources of useful information.

Becoming a Member of the Organization

When you start a new job, you are joining a team. Members of the team rely on each other in order to get their work done. As the new employee in the group, you should make an effort to get to know everyone by name: your peers, the supervisors, the secretaries, the technicians, the guards—everyone!

Building strong working relationships with your colleagues is different from developing personal friendships. Your co-workers do not need to know your life history to feel acquainted. Friendships with colleagues are built primarily on sharing work-related interests and activities. Time for conversation is limited during the working day, and you will want to make the most of opportunities to increase your understanding of who does what and how work gets done.

Learning Your Job

Your supervisor is the person who defines your job, assigns your work, and evaluates your performance. You will probably meet with him the first day and you should be prepared with questions that will clarify your responsibilities and his expectations. Your supervisor may be the person who trains you, or he may designate someone else to instruct you. If your supervisor is busy and does not have much time to help you get started, you should ask him whom you should turn to with your questions.

Every job has menial and repetitive work. Beware of thinking someone else should wait on you. You should be willing to undertake any of the tasks that are necessary to get the job done whether these be photocopying, word processing, or answering phones. Pitch in and do your part to help the team run smoothly.

Making a Commitment

Starting a new job is like moving to a foreign country. You have to learn the language, customs, and mores. You have to learn how to do your job. The first few weeks can be difficult. From time to time you may question whether this is the right job for you, but be patient. If your job represents a new challenge to you, you may not feel as if you are measuring up to your expectations for six months or a year. A challenging job takes a while to learn. Commit your best effort for a year and prove to yourself and your employer that you are worthy of his trust and respect.

Looking Ahead

If you have just completed a few weeks, months, or years engaged in exploring careers and conducting a job hunt, you have developed knowledge and skills that enable you to take charge of your own career. If career opportunities with your present employer do not meet your expectations, you know the process and have the skills for undertaking a new job hunt. If your talents and aspirations develop in such a way that your interest in your present career decreases, you know how to engage in career research to identify new and different possibilities. Tuned in to your own development and skilled in the career development process, you are prepared to forge your own career.

PLANNING YOUR FINANCES

Personal financial planning is the topic of numerous books, radio and television broadcasts, journal articles, workshops, and seminars. It is also a major industry: according to the *Encyclopedia of Associations*, the Institute of Certified Financial Planners has 7500 members nationwide and an annual budget of $2,600,000; the International Association for Financial Planning has 25,000 members in ten countries and a budget of $10,000,000! With so much attention being paid to the subject in the world at large, you may want to take a more personal view in terms of your own financial situation.

To begin with, the whole concept of financial planning revolves around one very basic tenet: what goes out must be less than or equal to what comes in. This sounds simple, but as anyone who has ever balanced a checkbook will tell you, there seem to be infinitely more ways to diminish one's cash on hand than to augment it. The negative numbers that are acceptable in the field of mathematics will not favorably impress your banker.

It is important to carefully examine and to anticipate what your actual expenses will be. This sounds easier than it is. Although you will be able to calculate your regular monthly costs with some accuracy, it is the occasional, unanticipated "extras" and the annual lump-sum payments for certain items that are guaranteed budget breakers. "Start-up" costs when establishing yourself in a new city or when building a professional wardrobe can also be disastrous to what you thought was the most carefully balanced budget.

Does this mean that you should begin searching for a wholesaler of red ink? Not quite. It does mean, however, that you need to be realistic when setting your priorities and when calculating what things really cost. You will also need to make sure you take into account just about anything that is likely to cost you money. The lists that follow are intended to help you do just that.

Monthly expenditures: housing (rent or mortgage and real estate tax payment, renter's/homeowner's insurance); utilities (electricity, gas, telephone, cable, water); heat/cooling (if not included in rent or utilities); transportation (public transportation, taxis, car rentals) or automobile expenses (monthly payment, insurance, parking, tolls, fuel/oil, excise tax, registration, car wash, routine maintenance); food; drycleaning/laundry; toiletries and household supplies; educational loans; entertainment (restaurants, movies, videotape rentals, sporting events, concerts, etc.); charitable contributions; postage (for paying all your bills!); etc.

Annual expenditures: professional memberships or dues; subscriptions; gifts (birthdays, anniversaries, etc.); annual credit card fees; travel (vacations, visits to friends/family, etc.).

In addition to the above, you need to realize that certain obligations will be met for you through payroll deductions: federal, state, and municipal taxes; social security or other preretirement contributions; health insurance premiums; any life/disability insurance or savings/supplemental pension plan through your employer.

By now you are probably wondering what is left and how to cover such "luxuries" as clothing for your new job or a few items to furnish your rather empty new living quarters (not to mention a couple of towels and an occasional bottle of champagne to celebrate your career advancement and that of your friends). One way to keep yourself reasonably solvent is to prioritize your expenditures, especially when you are starting out. You should also identify the items that are likely to take the biggest bite out of your resources (e.g., rent and transportation), and find ways to reduce them or keep them under control.

For instance, you may need to have several roommates to share housing and utility expenses or join a carpool rather than drive to work every day. Some employers will subsidize public transportation expenses; find out if this is an option where you work. Learn to shop for food and household supplies at supermarkets and discount stores rather than convenience stores and gourmet shops; you will pay less, especially if you watch for sales. Try to pay your credit card bills in full each month; otherwise, the finance charges will put a serious dent in your budget.

This is probably a good place to warn about the dangers of credit cards. It is very easy to place yourself in a great deal of debt in a very short period of time. Remember: that piece of plastic represents a commitment on your part to pay a bill. This bill will appear in your mailbox much sooner than you would like; to make matters worse, it will be accompanied by many others. That impulse purchase you made on your lunch hour will begin to transform itself into a millstone.

Last, but not least, you should get into the habit of saving a portion of each paycheck. The amount is not important, although the more you can set aside, the better your financial situation will be. A payroll deduction plan, if available to you, is a good way to insure that your good intentions in this regard become a reality.

Once you have begun the process of building a nest egg, you will be able to set longer-term financial goals and devise strategies to meet them. The process is the same whether you're saving for graduate school or for the downpayment on a house or a car: the money won't be there when you need it if you haven't put it there!

SOURCES

Resumes, Interviewing, Follow-up

Interview for Success, 3rd edition. Caryl Rae Krannich and Ronald L. Krannich. Impact Publications, Woodbridge, VA, 1990.
> Suggestions for making the most of an interview, with chapters on salary negotiation and follow-up. Sample letters and bibliography. Indexed.

Knock'em Dead with Great Answers to Tough Interview Questions. Martin John Yate. Bob Adams, Inc., Holbrook, MA, 1990.
> Strategies on how to get, survive, and follow up on the interview. Contains a bibliography and an index to the questions.

Liberal Arts Power! What It Is and How to Sell It on Your Resume, 2nd edition. Burton Jay Nadler. Peterson's Guides, Princeton, NJ, 1989.
> Includes sample resumes for a variety of backgrounds and objectives, as well as a separate section on cover letters.

Resumes that Work. Tom Cowan. New American Library, New York, NY, 1983.
> Sample resumes for different types of job seekers and career fields. Sample cover letters.

Sweaty Palms: The Neglected Art of Being Interviewed. H. Anthony Medley. Ten Speed Press, Berkeley, CA, 1984.
> A guide to the entire job-interview process from preparation to follow-up. Such topics as how to dress and salary discussions. Helpful appendixes on commonly asked questions, evaluation factors used by interviewers, questions asked by interviewers when they check your references. Bibliography.

Organizational Culture

Adventures in the Screen Trade: A Personal View of Hollywood and Screenwriting. William Goldman. Warner Books, New York, NY. 1983.
> A screenwriter's view of the Hollywood scene and the screenwriter's craft, with *Butch Cassidy and the Sundance Kid* as an example. A good introduction to a career field without many "how-to" manuals.

The Best Companies for Women. Baila Zeitz and Lorraine Dusky. Simon and Schuster, New York, NY, 1988.
> Profiles 50 companies with regard to their policies toward women, including excerpts from interviews with men and women in the companies. Draws some general conclusions in summary chapters. Appendixes list 60 additional companies worth investigating and index the profiled companies geographically (including branches). Name index.

Black Life in Corporate America: Swimming in the Mainstream. George Davis and Glegg Watson. Anchor Books, Garden City, NY, 1985.
> Examines corporate life from the perspective of black managers; contains interviews and quotes from individuals in various settings. Bibliography. Index.

The Black Manager: Making It in the Corporate World. Floyd Dickens, Jr., and Jacqueline B. Dickens. AMACOM, New York, NY, 1982.
> Written by management consultants, and intended as a handbook for blacks and other minorities in their corporate careers. Divided into four parts: "The Developmental Model;" "The Way to Success;" "Critical Guidelines for Success;" "Planning for Success." Contains a lot of information. Bibliography. Index.

Corporate Cultures: The Rites and Rituals of Corporate Life. Terrence E. Deal and Allan A. Kennedy. Addison-Wesley Publishing Co., Reading, MA, 1982.

> The title is self-explanatory: examines the corporate sphere in terms of its cultures, values, myths, symbols, and modes of communication. A good, interestingly written introduction to the corporate world. Bibliography. Index.

Fitting In: How to Get a Good Start in Your New Job. Natasha Josefowitz and Herman Gadon. Addison-Wesley Publishing Co., Inc., Reading, MA, 1988.

> Describes the process, with chapters on harrassment, organizational culture, relocation, etc. Indexed.

In Search of Excellence: Lessons from America's Best-Run Companies. Thomas J. Peters and Robert H. Waterman, Jr. Harper & Row, New York, NY, 1982.

> Examines successful companies and discusses what is likely to have made them that way. Indexed.

The 100 Best Companies to Work for in America. Robert Levering et al. Addison-Wesley Publishing Co., Reading, MA, 1984.

> Alphabetically lists and describes the companies, rating them in terms of pay, benefits, job security, advancement, and ambience. Gives one major advantage and one major disadvantage for each company, and ranks companies on just about any criterion you can think of. A lot of information!

Rating America's Corporate Conscience: A Provocative Guide to the Companies Behind the Products You Buy Every Day. Steven D. Lydenberg, Alice Tepper Marlin, and Sean O'Brien Strub. Addison-Wesley Publishing Co., Inc., Reading, MA, 1986.

> This publication of the Council on Economic Priorities provides information on the social responsibility records of major American companies, including policies relating to women, minorities, military contracts, PAC contributions, etc. Lists resources; summary list of company products and services. Indexed.

Reel Power: The Struggle for Influence and Success in the New Hollywood. Mark Litwak. New American Library, New York, NY, 1986.

> An insider's look at the film industry, including chapters on marketing, independent filmmaking, and Hollywood journalism. Based on interviews with 200 people in the business. Indexed.

Running from the Law: Why Good Lawyers are Getting Out of the Legal Profession. Deborah L. Arron. Niche Press, Seattle, WA, 1989.

> Based on interviews with successful practicing attorneys, this book includes profiles of individuals, career planning tips for lawyers, and an annotated list of resources.

This Business of Music, 5th edition. Sidney Shemel and M. William Krasilovsky. Billboard Publications, Inc., New York, NY, 1985.

Though not a job-search manual as such, this comprehensive treatment of business and legal issues in the recording, music, video, and related fields imparts a good sense of the "culture" of music. Lists additional sources of information.

Trading Up. Nancy Bazelon Goldstone. Dell, New York, NY, 1988.

A first-person account of currency options trading by one of the few women to run a Wall Street trading desk.

What They Still Don't Teach You at Harvard Business School. Mark H. McCormack. Bantam Books, New York, NY, 1989.

Practical advice on how to function and thrive in the business world. The sections "How to Find Your First Great Job (or What Every Graduate Wants to Know)," "Working for Nothing," and "What Really Happens to Resumes" are worth the price of the book!

Working in Foundations: Career Patterns of Women and Men. Teresa Jean Odendahl et al. The Foundation Center, New York, NY, 1985.

Written to study the status of women relative to men in the field of philanthropy, with a useful glimpse of the world of foundation work. Discusses recruitment and career paths.

Chapter 5

GRADUATE STUDY

CONSIDERING GRADUATE STUDY

As you learn about the world of work and assess your talents and interests in relation to the opportunities you find, you may choose a career goal that requires a graduate degree. It is not possible to be a lawyer without completing law school; it is not possible to be a doctor without completing medical school; if you want to pursue an academic career, you will need to earn a Ph.D.

Before you commit yourself to a career goal that requires graduate or professional school, it is best to spend time with professionals in several different areas within that field. Although you cannot engage in the practice of most professions before earning the required degree, it is possible to arrange to work closely with professionals and experience vicariously the opportunities, demands, and rewards of their work.

AN INTRODUCTION TO THREE PROFESSIONS

There are many career fields in which advanced professional study is required or preferred: for example, architecture, business, divinity, education, engineering, international relations, library and information science, mental health, and public policy. Selected references to assist you in beginning your exploration of these fields are listed in the "Index of Resources by Career Field" at the back of this book. In this chapter we will discuss briefly only three professions: academe, law, and medicine.

Academe

If you are reading this book while you are a college student, you have probably been in school all your life. If you have enjoyed your academic work and have done well, you may be thinking about academe as one of your career options.

Intellectual curiosity, enthusiasm for a particular field of study, and interest in independent inquiry are important factors in moving toward an academic career. Expanding the boundaries of knowledge; identifying new questions and seeking the answers; communicating your ideas through writing, speaking, and publishing; and sharing your knowledge with students are the central challenges in a career on the faculty of a college or university. Teaching is an integral part of the search for fuller understanding of the fundamental concepts and structure of your field. Interaction with students often generates new questions and insights.

If you are a college student, becoming involved in research with a professor in your major field of interest will enrich your education, and it will also give you the opportunity to learn whether you enjoy doing research. Reviewing the literature for your research papers will introduce you to various areas of study in the field. You may have already had teaching experience as a tutor, as a teaching assistant in high school or college, or as a friend to whom others come for assistance. Research and teaching introduce you to the activities of an academic career, but getting to know your professors well so that you can understand the satisfactions and rewards that they find in their careers will be most helpful in deciding whether you want to undertake a Ph.D. program.

Law

Lawyers take the role of advocate, negotiator, and adversary in their function as intermediaries between the law and the people. Whether his client is the government, a corporation, or an individual, the lawyer is responsible for interpreting the law to his client and for providing counsel on the legal issues related to specific decisions. The lawyer may initiate legal action on behalf of his client or undertake his client's defense if the client is accused of an illegal act. Lawyers in private practice assist individuals and organizations in understanding their rights and privileges within the law. Lawyers in public interest organizations work through the courts, the government, and the media to promote civil rights, arms control, protection of the environment, whatever their issues are. Lawyers working for the government have many responsibilities: legislation, interpretation, administration, and litigation.

The practice of law requires excellence in written and oral expression. Lawyers do a great deal of writing: the preparation of briefs which present a detailed defense of the client's position; the development of regulations for the implementation of legislation; the preparation of contracts, partnerships, wills, trusts, and other legal documents. Lawyers must be articulate in instructing their clients about the law, in litigating cases in court, in negotiating disputes.

Many kinds of work experience can give you insight into the legal profession. Working as a paralegal doing legal research provides the opportunity to work on legal problems, but so do many jobs for college graduates in the executive, legislative, or judicial branches of federal, state, or local government. Talking to lawyers in different types of practice will help you survey the variety of career opportunities in the field, as will *Choosing a Career in the Law*, *Practicing Law in New York City*, and *Career Preparation and Opportunities in International Law*. Reading publications such as *The National Law Journal* or the *ABA Journal* will give you a sense of what topics are important to lawyers.

Medicine

Medicine is a science-based helping profession. The basic responsibility of the physician is to treat people who are ill or in pain and to help people maintain good health. Most doctors spend all of their professional time seeing patients—and some of their personal time as well, when they respond to emergency calls. Some doctors conduct medical research and teach medical students and residents, but they also take care of patients.

There are many different specialties in medicine and many types of practice. The patients, the medical problems, the treatment modalities, and the patient interaction differ widely between psychiatry and surgery, between geriatrics and pediatrics. Choice of specialty is usually made during medical school, after clinical clerkships in each major specialty. Increasingly, doctors are practicing in clinics, health maintenance organizations, and other types of group practice. The number of physicians in private practice is expected to decrease steadily in the foreseeable future.

Spending time with a doctor while he is taking care of patients or making rounds, working with patients in a hospital as a volunteer or in a paid job, or being a research assistant on a medical research project are all ways to learn about the profession of medicine. Medical journals such as *American Medical News* are excellent sources of information on the important issues in the profession.

Other health professions that you may want to explore include dentistry, nursing, public health, and health policy and administration. The *Occupational Outlook Handbook* briefly describes professions and what graduate study is required. The VGM Professional Careers Series will introduce you to a variety of health care career options.

TAKING THE FIRST STEP

As you can see from the examples of academe, law, and medicine, the exploration process for career fields requiring advanced study follows the same pattern as that for fields one enters directly from a liberal arts background: reading the literature, interviewing and observing practioners, and gaining related paid or unpaid work experience. Ask yourself the same questions with regard to your personal preferences and priorities, relating them to the characteristics of the profession you are considering. Try to arrange opportunities to spend time with professionals in the field.

Reread Chapters 1 and 2, paying particular attention to the "Career Descriptive Literature" and "Directories of Career Literature and Counselors" sections of the bibliography at the end of Chapter 1. These resources will lead you to the journals and career literature for each field. To get started you might consult the "Index of Resources by Career Field" at the end of this book. For financial aid and graduate and professional school information, consult the resources that follow.

SOURCES

Graduate and Professional Education

AAA Guide: A Guide to Departments/A Directory of Members. American Anthropological Association. Washington, DC, annual.

Profiles anthropology departments in colleges and universities, community colleges, museums, research institutions, and government. Includes statistics on students and degree holders and a list of dissertations submitted during the year. Name and department indexes.

Admission Requirements of U.S. and Canadian Dental Schools. American Association of Dental Schools. Washington, DC, annual.

Discusses dentistry as a career, the dental school application process, and funding for dental education. Profiles dental schools, including admissions, curriculum, and financial information.

The American Film Institute Guide to College Courses in Film and Television, 8th edition. William Horrigan and Greg Beal, editors. ARCO, New York, NY, 1990.

Geographically profiles programs in the U.S. and Canada. Appendixes list foreign film and television schools, National Alliance of Media Arts Centers, and national and international organizations. Index of degrees offered, by state; general index to colleges.

The AWP Official Guide to Writing Programs, 5th edition. D. W. Fenza and Beth Jarock, editors. Associated Writing Programs, Old Dominion University, Norfolk, VA, 1990.

Profiles writing programs and their faculty in the U.S. and Canada; also describes writers' centers, colonies, and conferences, including one each in France, Ireland, and Italy. Geographic and degree indexes.

Directory of Graduate Programs. Graduate Record Examinations Board and the Council of Graduate Schools in the United States, Educational Testing Service, Princeton, NJ, annual. 4 volumes.

Tabular arrangement of U.S. graduate program information, including size of faculty and student body, degrees offered, admission requirements, and financial aid options. Supplemental information in narrative form arranged geographically.

Directory of Professional Preparation Programs in TESOL in the United States 1989-1991. Helen Kornblum with Margaret Gilligan. Teachers of English to Speakers of Other Languages, Inc., Alexandria, VA, 1989.

Provides basic information about college and university certificate and degree programs. Includes state certification requirements. Geographic index.

Directory of Theatre Training Programs. Jill Charles, compiler and editor. American Theatre Works, Inc., Dorset, VT, biennial.

Introductory articles on theater training, followed by geographic listings of college and conservatory programs. Includes information on admissions, degrees offered, faculty, courses, facilities, productions, and philosophy of training. Alphabetical index of institutions.

Educational Opportunities of Greater Boston for Adults: A Comprehensive Directory of Day and Evening Classes. The Educational Resource Institute (TERI), Boston, MA, annual.

Lists adult and continuing education courses throughout the metropolitan Boston area; includes schedules and costs.

Graduate Study in Psychology and Related Fields. American Psychological Association, Inc. Washington, DC, annual.

Four sections: departments and schools of psychology offering the doctoral degree; other departments offering the doctoral degree; graduate departments of psychology offering less than the doctoral degree; other graduate departments offering less than the doctoral degree. Area of study and institution indexes.

Guide to Architecture Schools in North America: Members and Affiliates of the ACSA. Richard E. McCommons, editor. Association of Collegiate Schools of Architecture Press, Washington, DC, 1989.

Introductory information on the field and on selecting an architecture school, followed by descriptions of schools, colleges, and departments of architecture. Includes a faculty roster and a list of schools of architecture worldwide.

The Independent Study Catalog: NUCEA's Guide to Independent Study Through Correspondence Instruction, 4th edition. John H. Wells and Barbara C. Ready, editors. Peterson's Guides for the National University Continuing Education Association, Princeton, NJ, 1989.

Alphabetical listing of institutions offering correspondence courses at the elementary, high school, vocational, college, and graduate levels, both credit and noncredit. Subject index.

Inside the Law Schools: A Guide by Students for Students, 4th edition. Sally F. Goldfarb. E.P. Dutton, New York, NY, 1986.

Profiles of law schools based on reports from students and recent graduates. Includes information on placement and on accessibility for disabled students.

The Insider's Guide to the Top Fifteen Law Schools. Cynthia L. Cooper. Doubleday, New York, NY, 1990.

Profiles each school in terms of academic environment, curriculum, extracurricular activities, social environment, facilities, the local community, admissions policies, and placement. Information is also provided in chart form for purposes of comparison.

The Insider's Guide to the Top Ten Business Schools, 4th edition. Tom Fischgrund, editor. Little, Brown and Co., Boston, MA, 1990.

Profiles programs on the basis of curriculum, admissions, academic environment, social life, and placement. Includes a general section on getting into, succeeding in, and doing well after business school. Comparision chart of the programs.

Medical School Admission Requirements. Association of American Medical Colleges. Washington, DC, annual.

Includes application information on medical schools in the United States and Canada, with introductory information on premedical planning. Financial aid information.

Mental Health Professions: A Guide to Graduate Education in Clinical Psychology, Counseling Psychology, Social Work. Martha P. Leape, revised by Patricia Walters. Office of Career Services and Off-Campus Learning, Harvard University, Cambridge, MA, 1984.

Introduces these fields and the education each requires. Includes bibliographic references throughout the text.

The Official Guide to U.S. Law Schools. Law School Admission Council/Law School Admission Services, Inc., Newtown, PA, annual.

Presents an overview of the legal profession, discusses the law school application process, and profiles ABA-approved law schools. Includes financial aid information.

Peterson's Annual Guides to Graduate Study. Peterson's Guides, Princeton, NJ, annual. 6 volumes.

Brief descriptions of accredited advanced degree programs in the U.S. and Canada, including application, financial aid, and program size information. Contact names and phone numbers are included; full-page descriptions of some programs.

The Preveterinary Planning Guide: Preparation Application and Admission Procedures to Veterinary (D.V.M.) Medical Colleges, 2nd edition. Jane Diehl Crawford. Betz Publishing Co., Bethesda, MD, 1990.

Includes chapters on planning career-related experiences and other options for unsuccessful applicants. Bibliography. Indexed.

Rx: A Prescription for Medicine: A Premedical Guide. Hope W. Wigglesworth. The Office of Career Services, Harvard University, Cambridge, MA, 1986.

Opens with an overview of the profession and medical education. Discusses requirements, application process, funding, and opportunities for minorities. Identifies other health careers. A "Premedical Checklist" is particularly useful, outlining the timing of various phases of the medical school application process. The selected readings and bibliography should be required reading for anyone contemplating medicine as a career.

Survey of Arts Administration Training. Center for Arts Administration, Graduate School of Business, University of Wisconsin-Madison and Association of Arts Administration Educators. ACA Books, New York, NY, biennial.

Profiles programs in the U.S. and Canada. Includes a list of job placement services.

Veterinary Medical School Admission Requirements in the United States and Canada. Marcia James Sawyer. Betz Publishing Co., Inc., Bethesda, MD, annual.

Sponsored by the Association of American Veterinary Medical Colleges, this geographically arranged directory includes application and enrollment data, information on combined degree and other special programs, and financial aid information.

Who Offers Part-Time Degree Programs? 2nd edition. Peterson's Guides, Princeton, NJ, 1985.

Includes daytime, evening, weekend, summer, and external degree programs at both the undergraduate and graduate levels.

Financial Aids and Grants

Annual Register of Grant Support: A Directory of Funding Sources. National Register Publishing Co., Wilmette, IL, annual.

Nonrepayable financial support programs, arranged by subject, with separate sections for international studies and special applicant populations (Black, Native American, Spanish-speaking, women). Eligibility and application information. Subject, organization/program, geographical, and personnel indexes.

Foundation Annual Reports.

Many foundations issue publicly obtainable annual reports. These reports account for the history, purpose, function, and current activities of the foundation, and can provide valuable information for the grant seeker. Each issue of *The Foundation Grants Index Quarterly,* published by the Foundation Center, New York, NY, contains a list of publications, including annual reports, available from grantmakers.

The Foundation Directory. The Foundation Center, New York, NY, annual.

Provides information on the nation's largest foundations. The subject and type of support (for example, "grants to individuals") indexes are quite useful. Identifies publicly accessible reference collections throughout the U.S.

Foundation Grants to Individuals, 6th edition. The Foundation Center, New York, NY, 1988.

Lists foundation grant programs for individuals (as opposed to those aimed at institutional support). Foundation, subject, types of support, geographic focus, company employee grant, and specific educational institution indexes.

The Grants Register. St. Martin's Press, Inc., New York, NY, biennial.

Intended primarily for students at or above the graduate level, the register lists scholarships, fellowships, research grants, competitions, prizes, and special awards. Includes eligibility and application information.

Money for Artists: A Guide to Grants and Awards for Individual Artists. Laura R. Green, editor. American Council for the Arts, New York, NY, 1987.

Arranged in five sections: literary arts, media arts, multidisciplinary arts, performing arts, and visual arts. Awards, organization, geographic, and artistic discipline indexes. Includes artist-in-residence programs.

Peterson's Grants for Graduate Students 1989-90, 2nd edition. John H. Wells and Amy J. Goldstein, editors. Peterson's Guides, Princeton, NJ, 1989.

Contains an introduction to the grant-seeking process, followed by an alphabetical list of grant and fellowship programs. Fields of study, special eligibility requirements, and administering agency indexes. Selected bibliography.

Scholarships & Grants for Study or Research in USA: A Scholarship Handbook for Foreign Nationals. American Collegiate Service, Houston, TX, 1989.

Describes the funding process and lists sources of financial aid, from the undergraduate to the postdoctoral level. Bibliography. Indexed.

State Foundation Directories.

Directories of private foundations registered with the state as charitable, tax-exempt institutions are available for most states; these are helpful in identifying smaller foundations not accounted for in other sources like *The Foundation Directory*.

Supporting Yourself as an Artist: A Practical Guide, 2nd edition. Deborah A. Hoover. Oxford University Press, New York, NY, 1989.

Discusses the various ways in which artists can identify sources of financial support, as well as the types of support available (prizes, residencies, internships, etc.). Includes chapters on proposal writing and the review process. Appendixes on resume preparation and organizations cited within the text. Glossary and bibliography. Indexed.

USE OF THE CAREER BIBLIOGRAPHIES

This appendix is designed as an aid to the use of the many volumes cited in the Sources at the end of each chapter. The first section is an index of the most important volumes to use as resources for certain career fields; the second is a complete listing of all titles cited in the book. In both cases the pages on which the pertinent bibliographic information may be found are indicated.

The selected career areas for which information is given are the following:

Advertising/Public Relations	Information Systems
Architecture	Insurance
Banking/Finance	Law
Consulting	Manufacturing/Production
Education	Marketing/Sales
Government	Media/Publishing/Entertainment
Health/Medicine	Public Interest
Hospitality	Real Estate
Human Resource Management/	Science and Technology
Training and Development	Trade/Transportation/Travel
Human Services	Visual and Performing Arts

The listing for each field includes books that have a chapter devoted to that field. Excluded are the more comprehensive descriptive materials that cover virtually the entire range of career options: *The American Almanac of Jobs and Salaries*, the Catalyst Career Opportunity Series, the *Occupational Outlook Handbook*, the VGM Opportunities Series, and the VGM Professional Careers Series, for example. (These are listed in the "Career Descriptive Literature" section of the bibliography for Chapter 1.) Also excluded from the Appendix listing are professional journals and well-known general indexes such as those to the *Wall Street Journal* and the *New York Times*.

INDEX OF RESOURCES BY CAREER FIELD

Advertising/Public Relations

Architecture

Banking/Finance

Consulting

Education

Government

Health/Medicine

Hospitality

Human Resource Management/Training & Development

Human Services

Information Systems

Insurance

Law

Manufacturing/Production

Marketing/Sales

Media/Publishing/Entertainment

Public Interest

Trade/Transportation/Travel

Visual and Performing Arts

INDEX OF TITLES